D0871892

JOHN BARRETT
PROGRESSIVE ERA DIPLOMAT

John Barrett,
Progressive Era Diplomat:
A Study of a Commercial Expansionist,
1887-1920

BY

SALVATORE PRISCO III

THE UNIVERSITY OF ALABAMA PRESS
University, Alabama 35486

For:
DOROTHY *and* LISA

Contents

Acknowledgments

I wish to thank the Research Grants Committee of the University of Alabama for a Grant-in-Aid to revise this study which began as a doctoral dissertation at Rutgers University. To the Windham Foundation of Vermont I extend my appreciation for a grant which made possible the completion of this book. I would like to thank the library staffs at the Manuscript Division of the Library of Congress, the National Archives, the Bancroft Library of the University of California at Berkeley, the New York City Public Library, the Rutgers University Library, the Princeton University Library, and the Gorgas Library of the University of Alabama for their assistance and cooperation.

To Professor Lloyd C. Gardner of Rutgers University, I express my sincere appreciation; for this study was dependent upon his suggestions, guidance, and encouragement. To Professors Warren I. Susman and Gerald Pomper of Rutgers University, Dean David A. Shannon of the University of Virginia, and Professor Robert A. Waller of the University of Illinois, I am indebted for valuable critiques.

Portions of this book are printed in revised form from articles appearing in *Vermont History*, the *Oregon Historical Quarterly*, and *The Americas*.

Tuscaloosa, Alabama   SALVATORE PRISCO III
May, 1973

vi

Preface

THE decade of the 1970's will be a time of soul-searching for the United States as it examines the failure of some of its policies designed to create stable, democratic, free-enterprise systems in Latin America and the Far East. Many of these policies were formulated in the period 1890 to 1920, when all things seemed possible for a nation dedicated to the idea of material progress, and earnestly committed to spreading its gospel to underdeveloped countries. To understand better how the policies of the United States were drawn up in this period, it will be necessary for historians to look beyond the traditional scope of diplomatic history, and to seek out individuals and influences heretofore overlooked.

One such individual was John Barrett (1866–1938), a career diplomat and commercial publicist. As an American minister in the Far East (1894–1898) and Latin America (1904–1906), and Director General of the Pan American Union (1907–1920), Barrett has long been a footnote to larger studies of American commercial expansion and foreign relations at the end of the nineteenth century. Walter Millis, writing in *The Martial Spirit*, noted Barrett's role as a commercial publicist who argued for the greater participation of the United States in Asian affairs after the capture of the Philippines in the war with Spain.[1]

Charles S. Campbell Jr., in *Special Business Interests and the Open Door Policy*, described John Barrett as "An enthusiastic and persistent advocate of America's mission in the Pacific, [who] had influence which seems to have been comparable to Clarence Cary's although less than John Foord's.[2] In *The New Empire*, Walter

LaFeber noted Barrett's activities to expand American exports to Japan while he was United States Minister to Siam (1894–1898).[3] Recently, Thomas McCormick has remarked in his study, *China Market: America's Quest for Informal Empire, 1893–1901,* that

> The role of foreign service personnel has been largely ignored, though it is clear to me that people like Charles Denby, Charles Denby Jr., John Barrett and Thomas Jernigan exercised an impact upon Far Eastern affairs even beyond the capacity of their positions.[4]

Although Barrett's papers have long been available to scholars, he remains a minor character in diplomatic studies.[5] Placed in proper perspective, however, Barrett's career as a commercial publicist and diplomat reveals important information about aspects of American commercial expansion and diplomacy in the Progressive Era. In 1911 former American Ambassador to China Paul S. Reinsch defined the Progressive Era diplomat with these words:

> A successful diplomat today must master the intricate organization and interaction of world wide industrial, commercial, and scientific forces which give to national life a new and broader significance.[6]

Few diplomats tried harder to fulfill this description than did John Barrett.

A child of the industrial age, John Barrett grew up believing in the positive, scientific development of all facets of modern industrial society resulting in the most efficient use of resources and production. Within his world view, American commercial expansion into the underdeveloped areas of the world was to be an integral part of this movement for industrial efficiency and progress.[7] Before long, Barrett was able to realize his beliefs and his own career goals in the commercial and political opportunities of the United States in the Far East and Latin America.

The pattern of John Barrett's life in his productive years, 1890 to 1920, was such that it virtually paralleled the expansion of the United States on two levels—first, to the geographical western frontier, and second, to the commercial frontier westward across the Pacific in the Far East and to the south in Latin America. Extraor-

dinarily perceptive at an early age to the importance of the impact
of industrialism on American life, Barrett chose to make himself
an integral part of the age in which he lived, an age of commercial
expansion and industrial, technological, and human progress.

Driven by a strong personal need to succeed, especially in order
to gain his mother's recognition and praise, young Barrett considered
careers in law and the ministry. After probing for opportunities in
New England and the New South, he seized upon the directive to
"go west!" as the key to the kingdom of success. But his arrival
in California in 1890 coincided with the announcement that the
western frontier no longer existed. Although the Pacific loomed large
before him, Barrett never thought of it as a confining border, but
instead as an avenue to real success.

The Pacific Northwest was a region just beginning to exhibit its
industrial and commercial might before the nation and the world.
Here was a genuine opportunity for fame and fortune. Under the
influence of west coast journalists and businessmen, John Barrett
became a stalwart proponent of American commercial expansion into
Asia and Latin America. His major work as a commercial publicist
was done in the interest of Oregon and Washington businessmen.
Eventually he became, in effect, the promotion man for the financial
and industrial empire of William S. Ladd and Theodore B. Wilcox.
But in a general way, Barrett's work for commercial expansion served
the commercial interests of the Pacific Northwest and the entire
American business community as a whole.

Rising through the ranks of the Oregon Democratic Party after
campaigning for the reelection of Grover Cleveland to the Presidency
in 1892, John Barrett was designated by the commercial interests
and politicians of the Northwest for a diplomatic patronage position
in the Far East. His subsequent appointment as Minister to Siam
not only repaid loyal Democrats in the Pacific Northwest but provided
Barrett with the opportunity he had been seeking.

From his post in Siam, Barrett called for increased American
involvement throughout Asia in order to compete with the imperial
policies of other nations. This involvement had two facets. In the

first place he called upon American businessmen themselves to seize the opportunity to expand their trade in Asia. In the second instance he requested that the State Department do all in its power to support commercial expansion. Thus Barrett, and others like him in the diplomatic corps, provided a vital link between the business community and the State Department.

Although often holding secondary positions, these members of the diplomatic corps contributed significantly to the formulation of American foreign policy. They represented a new generation of American diplomats in an age of mass industrial and economic progress. In addition to John Barrett, they included such men as Julean Arnold, Consul General in Shanghai; Charles Denby Sr., Minister to China; Charles Denby Jr., Secretary of the American Legation in Peking; Mark Dunnell, Deputy Consul General at Shanghai; Paul S. Reinsch, Ambassador to China; Thomas Jernigan, Consul General in Osaka, Hiago, and Shanghai; John Van Antwerp MacMurray, Secretary of the American Legation in Bangkok and Peking, and later Assistant Secretary of State; Willys Peck, Secretary of the American Legation in Peking; Willard Straight, Consul General in Mukden, Manchuria; E. T. Williams, Chief of the Far Eastern Division of the State Department; Francis B. Loomis, Minister to Venezuela and Assistant Secretary of State; Horace Allen, Minister to Korea; and Edwin H. Conger, Minister to Brazil and China.

This study is concerned primarily with one of these men, John Barrett. It is not a biography of the man, but rather a study of his career as a commercial publicist and diplomat in the Progressive Era. As a representative of the new generation of American diplomats, John Barrett serves as a "concrete universal." This new generation sought to expand the commercial and political influence of the United States in the Far East and Latin America according to the broadly conceived progressive economic tenets of industrial efficiency and commercial expansion. John Barrett was a zealous exponent of this creed.

Faith in the ability of the United States to respond effectively to the economic, social, and political problems resulting from the impact of industrialism on American society was a noteworthy characteristic of the Progressive Era. John Barrett exhibited deep faith in the ability of the United States not only to solve its own problems, but to provide a solution for other nations as well. In the long run, Barrett believed, American leadership in the commercial development of the waste places of the earth was of paramount importance for the continuance of a healthy, expansive industrial society in the United States, and the first step in the modern progressive development of other areas of the world. With foreign markets and overseas industrial and commercial development, all classes in the United States could look forward to full employment, economic prosperity, and social stability. Although this interpretation provided an oversimplified answer to the problems of a society trying to respond to the impact of industrialism, John Barrett hoped to make this conception of American society a blueprint for world progress.

These ideas eventually became part of the basis of American policies in Latin America and the Far East. This was not primarily because Barrett believed in them and worked for their acceptance, but because they appeared to provide answers to the perplexing problems of maintaining domestic prosperity and providing for the growth of the United States as a world power. John Barrett was a finished product of the age in which he lived. In his beliefs, accomplishments, and failures, one can find operative some of the underlying assumptions of American foreign policy in the twentieth century.

JOHN BARRETT
PROGRESSIVE ERA DIPLOMAT

1. *Genesis of*
A Progressive Era Diplomat
1887–1894

INSIGHT into the highly complex world of the Progressive Era came to John Barrett while he was still an undergraduate at Dartmouth College. Early in life Barrett became personally committed to the development of the new American industrial society. The world of 1890 was quite large and full of frontiers to conquer. John Barrett's nature was such that he could not allow himself to bypass a challenge. The New South, the West, the Pacific frontier stimulated his imagination and ambition. The United States was on the threshold of a new era. Industry, science, and commerce held the keys to the future. But not everyone had insight into the progression of American civilization. First as a newspaperman and publicist, and then as a diplomat, John Barrett sought to widen the circle of awareness.

The role that ideas and ideals played in formulating the attitudes of the young John Barrett is significant for an understanding of his subsequent career. The influence of three individuals was important in this respect: James G. Blaine, Henry W. Grady, and Caroline Sanford Barrett.

The ideas of Secretary of State James G. Blaine became meaningful for Barrett as early as 1887.[1] As a member of the Dartmouth debating team, Barrett was continually searching for suitable material. He had been particularly impressed with two of Blaine's recently published books, *Twenty Years of Congress, 1861–1881*, and *Political Discussions: Legislative, Diplomatic, and Popular, 1856–1886.*[2]

These works contained many of Blaine's ideas concerning the role that the government should play in expanding American commerce. Among these were suggestions for government promotion of commerce through direct aid to private corporations, and the need for a revived American merchant marine. Blaine anticipated that the expansion of American commerce would result in the predominance of the United States commercially, and ultimately politically, in both the Pacific area and Latin America. The capstone of Blaine's program was his plan for a union of the nations of the western hemisphere to promote peace and commerce. To implement this plan, Blaine eventually became a champion of reciprocal trade agreements.[3]

Over the years, John Barrett quietly absorbed Blaine's ideas and proposals within his own world view. Subsequently he was able to publicize them and work for their realization as a personal representative of American commercial expansion.[4]

Another individual who left his mark upon Barrett was Henry W. Grady, the Southern journalist, orator, and commercial publicist. In 1887, Barrett had selected Grady's address before the New England Society in New York City (1886) entitled "The New South" as his topic in a college speech contest.[5] This speech had a profound effect upon him. In it Grady spoke of the South as a land "thrilling with new life" as a result of the rapid diversification of crops and industries:

> There is a New South, not through protest against the Old, but because of new conditions, new adjustments and . . . new ideas and aspirations.. . . We have sowed towns and cities in the place of theories, and put business above politics. We have challenged your spinners in Massachusetts and your iron makers in Pennsylvania. . . . We have fallen in love with work. . . . In the record of her social, industrial and political illustrations we await with confidence the verdict of the world.
>
> The Old South rested everything on slavery and agriculture, unconscious that these could neither give nor maintain healthy growth. The New South presents a perfect Democracy . . . a hundred farms for every

plantation, fifty homes for every palace, and a diversified industry that meets the complex needs of this complex age. . . . The New South is enamoured of her new work. . . . She is thrilling with the consciousness of a growing power and prosperity.[6]

The only way for the South to regain power and prosperity in the post-Civil War period was for it to welcome Northern industrialism and make it an integral part of its own development. The factory was essential to Southern prosperity. As early as 1874 Grady had recognized this, and said that the New South needed enterprising men with ability to foster commercial growth.[7]

In a later speech in Dallas, Texas (1889), Grady portrayed the post-war South as a new frontier for industry and commerce:

> The pioneer has now replaced the soldier. Commerce has widened new seas, and the merchant has occupied new areas. Steam has made the earth a chessboard on which men play for markets. . . . There is competition everywhere.[8]

Grady believed that from defeat the South would rise to victory in the battle for international markets through the expansion of its industrial potential.

Such statements started young Barrett thinking of the New South as a land of opportunity. As in the case of Comfort Servosse, the protagonist of Albion W. Tourgee's famous novel, *A Fool's Errand,* John Barrett concluded that an industrialized South offered a young man a chance to become a new pioneer.[9] The growth of the Southern iron industry had imparted the spirit of enterprise with abundant promises for the South's future. All of American society had come to the threshold of a new industrial and technological frontier, and John Barrett wanted to be an integral part of it.

In addition to the writings of publicists, there was another influence in Barrett's life that directed his interests toward the South. This was Caroline Sanford Barrett, his mother. Caroline Barrett had been a teacher in Alabama and Tennessee before the Civil War and still had relatives in Knoxville. Barrett's memory of his mother's tales of life in the South during the long cold nights on their Grafton, Vermont farm gave the region a romantic significance for him. From the correspondence which they carried on throughout Barrett's child-hood and adult life, it is evident that she influenced his outlook to an extraordinary degree.[10]

Caroline Barrett was a sophisticated and self-confident woman who had taken a lively interest in a broad range of subjects. Politics, journalism, law, theology, and economics fascinated her. She provided a vital example to her son. By comparison, Barrett's father, Charles, was a shy, withdrawn man. He was a descendant from old New England stock, and a Son of the American Revolution. He had been a Republican Vermont state legislator as his father had been before him. But his great interest was art, and he soon left politics to open a studio in Boston. Young Barrett's knowledge of his father's shyness and lack of worldly ambition led him to look upon his father as a failure, and disposed him to emulate his mother. Throughout his adult life, Barrett faithfully told his mother how certain he was of himself and the great things he would accomplish in life.[11]

Forearmed with the concepts of Henry W. Grady and James G. Blaine, and forewarned by the strong sense of self-awareness imparted by his mother, John Barrett decided to make a career in the legal profession and practice law in the New South. To this end, he applied for admission to Vanderbilt University in Nashville, Tennessee for a year's study, 1887–1888. There he studied political economy and international law. But the greatest influence on Barrett at Vanderbilt was the Presbyterian ministry, and a new vocation was opened to his mission-oriented idealism. He decided that he would enter the ministry after graduating from Dartmouth. He thought he might teach for a year or two and then enter a first class seminary. He was explicit about wanting the best.[12]

Barrett considered going South the turning point in his life. It seemed to him "almost providential." [13] New vistas of America's development had been opened to him by Grady's writings. Despite his enthusiasm for the South, however, Barrett decided not to seek his fortune there. At Vanderbilt he had observed that the South was already populated with capable young men. Thus it was not surprising that Barrett chose to follow Horace Greeley's advice and "go west."

A Vermont friend arranged a teaching position for Barrett at Hopkins Academy in Oakland, California after he graduated from Dartmouth in 1889. The sparsely settled West offered even greater opportunities than the New South. Everything that was true of the South concerning its future development was just as true of the West. But there was one major exception—the West was completely wide open to men with ability who were intent on "getting there." There were no chains to the past. The modern development of California, Oregon, and Washington was certain in Barrett's mind. Providence, he believed, brought him west as it once had brought him south.[14]

Shortly after arriving on the Pacific coast Barrett, who was an enterprising individual by nature, became enthusiastic about the growth potential of the region and tried to interest his father in land speculation at Gray's Harbor, Washington. He told his father of the great lumber industry, the modern railway transportation, and the potentially great harbor facilities for export trade. To the ambitious younger Barrett, "God never made a harbor not to be utilized."[15]

The elder Barrett, however, was not persuaded so easily, and decided against making the investment. His son took his refusal personally. He felt that his father thought him too young and optimistic to understand such matters. At age twenty-three John Barrett thought of the West, in his own words, as a whole "new empire" where the man with drive could reach boundless heights.[16] Barrett was in fact describing himself when he wrote to his father

But I state a *positive fact* when I say that there is a splendid, noble, minority of young men *not over* 23 years old who are controlling vast interests, making excellent investments, starting and managing responsible businesses, well deserving the confidence of their fellows, well earning the respect of older men, courageously proving that though they may be but 23 they can succeed, plan, guide, and think as well as those who carry 43, 53, or 63 years. . . . The old prejudice against young men is dying becuase it *must*. . . . Let me have health and no severe accident befall me, and I mean to have something accomplished worthy of the name within the next ten years. This is the country to do it in. It may not be money—but it will be influence at least and position, which are pretty sure to bring money.[17]

Thoughts of the ministry faded in the wake of tempting opportunities in the West. While still teaching, Barrett secured a part-time position as a writer and editor for L. P. McCarty's *Annual Statistician and Economist*, which was described as a "cyclopedia handbook" of world knowledge. Shortly thereafter Barrett decided to leave teaching, and devote his full energy to journalism.

His first job was that of a reporter for the San Francisco *Chronicle*. His assignment was to write "boom" articles to promote west coast development. Under the tutelage of the *Chronicle's* editor and founder, Michael de Young, Barrett received the basic training for a career as a commercial publicist.[18] De Young was to be vice-president of the World's Columbia Exposition National Commission in 1892, commission-general from California to the Trans-Mississippi Exposition at Omaha in 1898, and vice-president of the Panama-Pacific International Exposition in 1915.

As a writer of "boom" articles, Barrett came into contact with a great many commercial interests, and his work as a promotion man was soon in demand. Developing west coast communities were engaged in heated competition to entice settlers and capital. A talented pen was indispensable to such communities, and he quickly found that his own gave him opportunity for the advancement that he sought. In 1890 he left San Francisco for a better position as assistant editor of *The Astorian*, an Oregon daily.[19] Later in the same year he was hired by Samuel Pettengill, a fellow Vermonter from Grafton, as city editor of the more influential Tacoma *Daily Ledger*.

In 1891 Barrett received his biggest break. Harvey W. Scott, editor of the strongest Republican paper in the Pacific Northwest, the Portland *Morning Oregonian*, had decided that the lack of competition from a good Democratic newspaper would lead eventually to the establishment of one. He hoped to avoid this possibility by putting the floundering Democratic daily, the Portland *Evening Telegram*, on a solid foundation. Outwardly the Democratic *Telegram* and the Republican *Oregonian* would appear to be in competition. Actually they would be expounding a similar viewpoint.[20]

Scott's choice to run the *Telegram* had to be a "boomer" for Oregon and the Pacific coast like himself. He had to be someone who was interested in low tariffs and commercial expositions. Scott himself was to be president of the Lewis and Clark Exposition in Portland in 1905. John Barrett was an excellent choice for the position, but there was one obstacle—Barrett was a Republican. Scott proposed that he become a Democrat, and Barrett did not hesitate to follow his advice.[21] After all, changing parties did not necessarily entail changing philosophies. Thus Barrett became editor of the Portland *Evening Telegram* and a Democrat all at the same time.

Barrett not only ran a nominally Democratic newspaper, he joined the Oregon party, and shortly thereafter was chosen chairman of the Young Men's Democratic Club of Portland. In this capacity, he came into personal association with Oregon commercial interests. Two men in particular emerged very early in this group—Vermont-born financier William S. Ladd and his associate Theodore B. Wilcox.[22]

William S. Ladd was a principal merchant in the Pacific Northwest. His holdings included the Ladd and Tilton Bank, the Oregon Steam and Navigation Company, Oregon Railway and Navigation Company, Oregon Iron and Steel Company, Oregon Central Railroad, Oregon Telegraph Company, and the Portland Flouring Mills, the largest manufacturing corporation in the Northwest. Ladd also manufactured furniture and cordage.[23]

Theodore B. Wilcox, a staunch advocate of expanding American markets in Asia, was president of the Portland Flouring Mills, director of the Pacific Coast Steamship Company, and a director of the Ladd and Tilton Bank and the First National Bank of Portland.[24] Eventually John Barrett became a kind of promotion man for the Ladd-Wil-

cox financial, shipping, and industrial empire, and in a general way
for the commercial interests of the Pacific Northwest. It was Theodore
Wilcox who later became Barrett's chief sponsor for a diplomatic
post in Asia.

With these connections, Barrett quickly worked his way up in
the ranks of the Oregon Democratic Party. In 1892 he was chosen
to be a delegate to the Democratic National convention in Chicago.
Although he was unable to attend the Convention because of commit-
ments to the *Telegram*, he had already given his full support to
the nomination of Grover Cleveland for President, and Cleveland's
promise of a downward revision of the tariff.[25]

With the election of Cleveland, Barrett and his Oregon associates
looked forward to significant decreases in tariff duties and a new
growth in exports. The subsequent Wilson-Gorman Tariff of 1894
did provide lower average tariff rates than the act it was designed
to replace—39.9 per cent to the McKinley Tariff's 48.4 per cent—but
it was still a high protective tariff. Although President Cleveland
did not support the measure, he allowed it to become law without
his signature. It did, after all, provide moderate tariff reform.

Democratic and Republican commercial interests in Oregon, however, were dissatisfied with this policy. While many pressure groups
in the United States insisted upon high tariffs to protect the domestic
market, Oregon commercial interests generally sought an approach
to trade that would provide Asian and Latin American markets for
their products.[26] This meant the necessity of lower tariffs. But in
addition, Northwestern businessmen hoped to promote the export
trade of their section by the appointment of a forceful diplomatic
agent to represent them in the Far East.[27]

Their arguments for the selection of a diplomatic representative
did not rest on patronage alone. They also feared that foreign competitors, long active in the quest for Asian markets, would win all
the markets for themselves, and effectively exclude American commerce. Thus they argued that the selection of capable men for the
diplomatic corps of the United States who were knowledgeable in

many broad areas, and especially in matters of commerce, served the national interest as well as particular sectional economic interests.

In 1893 the consularship of Kanagawa, Japan was vacant. Pacific coast businessmen and politicians designated John Barrett as the man they wanted for the post. In his application to the State Department, Barrett explained that he should be awarded the Kanagawa consularship as a spokesman for the Pacific Northwest "because of allied commercial interests, and because an Eastern man cannot appreciate the great importance of this trans-Pacific trade [to the Pacific Northwest] and would not especially exert himself to build it up." [28]

In support of Barrett's candidacy, letters of recommendation from diverse interests were written to congressmen, the State Department, and the President. Theodore B. Wilcox wrote to Oregon Representative Joseph N. Dolph that he was planning to expand the Portland Flouring Mills into the Japanese trade and needed an agent to represent him. In 1890 San Francisco had controlled the flour market, but Portland and Tacoma had begun shipping via the Northern Pacific and Canadian Pacific steamship companies, and had taken over a good portion of the trade. Wilcox concluded his recommendation by stating:

> While Mr. Barrett's official duties would not permit him to serve us except in a general way, he could be of great service to us in developing this trade [flour] which is, in the matter of tonnage, the most important item shipped from this coast to Japan.[29]

Magnus Crosby, mayor of Astoria, in a letter to Secretary of State Walter Q. Gresham, described Barrett as a "progressive, energetic and trustworthy individual" who could best serve the commercial interests of the Pacific coast.[30] The president of Ladd and Bush Bankers of Salem, Oregon expressed similar thoughts.[31] Recommendations also came from the Jefferson Democratic Club of Oregon, the Federated Trades Assembly of Portland and the Oregon Pacific Railroad Company.[32]

The president of the Young Men's Democratic League of Portland wrote to President Cleveland:

> The sending of a representative to Japan from this state would be a recognition of increasing and important commercial relations. In the last campaign Mr. Barrett was continually on the stump in Oregon, and to some extent in Washington and California. He represents the progressive democracy of the Pacific coast.[33]

Oregon Democratic State Chairman D. R. Murphy, National Committeeman E. D. McKee, Portland Chamber of Commerce President Markle, and Portland Mayor William S. Mason expressed similar sentiments to Assistant Secretary of State Josiah Quincy:

> The young progressive and Cleveland element of the party here are united in our endorsement and the older conservative element of both parties . . . earnestly lend their approbation.[34]

In addition to their recommendation of Barrett, these men voiced the fear that foreign domination of Japanese markets would be disastrous for the United States and West coast commerce. In order to counteract this threat and enhance the chances of American expansion into Japanese markets, they noted that such corporations as the Oregon Pacific, the Northern Pacific and the Southern Pacific railroads, and the First National Bank of Portland had decided to support John Barrett for the consular post.[35]

When news was received that a Mr. McIvor of Iowa was given the Kanagawa appointment as a result of party patronage, Oregon businessmen deemed their commercial future so bound up in Japanese trade that they promptly and energetically endorsed Barrett for the consularship of Osaka, Japan. Letters and telegrams were again sent to the President and State Department. Theodore B. Wilcox together with Charles E. Ladd and Henry Failing of the First National Bank of Portland wrote to President Cleveland that "Japan with its 41,000,000 population and consequent possible demands offers an extensive field of export from the Pacific coast, and, in fact, from all the United States." [36] Washington and California were already represented in the consular service; now Oregon required her agent.

In his campaign to marshall support for the Osaka appointment, Barrett wrote to Peter Studebaker, the manufacturer of farm machinery, whom he had met the year before, requesting his endorsement. Barrett stated his role clearly when he wrote "I want to wake up the United States to the opportunity of the trans-Pacific commerce. I am not looking for a 'soft' job, but a chance to make a name as a developer of great opportunities." [37] Barrett argued that if the United States did not make its move, England, France, and Germany would take all the Asian markets for themselves. Studebaker was convinced and subsequently endorsed Barrett to Secretary of State Gresham.[38]

Despite this solid support from men such as Wilcox, Studebaker, and even Vermont Senator Redfield Proctor,[39] Barrett was denied a Japanese post for a second time. With this refusal, Wilcox decided that the only way to acquire a consular post in Asia for the business interests of Oregon and the Pacific Northwest was to finance Barrett on a trip to Washington, D.C. so that he could make a personal pitch to President Cleveland.[40]

When Barrett arrived in Washington, he found that there were no longer any openings left in Japan, but through a friend in the Democratic Party in Washington, Josephus Daniels, he managed to get an introduction to Assistant Secretary of State Josiah Quincy. Years later Daniels recalled the episode:

> Barrett, young and attractive, favorably impressed Quincy. I didn't see Barrett after that for some days, and was gratified and astonished one morning to pick up the *Washington Post* and read the headlines: JOHN BARRETT HAS BEEN APPOINTED MINISTER TO SIAM! Knowing that he had not aspired higher than a consulate, I asked him what rabbit foot he had used to get the place. It seems he had made a study of Siam and its trade in connection with his newspaper work. . . . For some reason he spoke of that to Quincy and later Cleveland sent to the State Department for some information about Siam. Quincy recalled what Barrett had told him about Siam and told the President, "I will ask John Barrett to call and he can give you the information." As a result of the call, and because he could give Cleveland exactly what he wanted at the time, the President offered him the position of Minister

to Siam. It was a godsend to the ambitious young journalist who had begun to despair of securing a government position.[41]

At age twenty-seven at the time of his appointment (February 13, 1894), John Barrett became the youngest minister in American history. Oregon commercial interests at last had the spokesman they wanted in the Far East.

Shortly after Barrett underwent important State Department briefings for his post, he received the first in a series of significant communications from the Siamese Consul-General in New York, Isaac Townsend Smith, a fellow American, concerning American economic relations with Siam and all of Asia.[42] Smith called attention to the fact that the United States needed foreign markets for its surplus production and as sources for vital raw materials just as the European imperial powers:

> The United States needs the friendship of Siam; we are becoming a great manufacturing nation and foreign markets are absolutely necessary for an output of our fabrics. Siam is an agricultural country and can take many things made in the United States. If therefore the Siamese markets can be kept open for us, we shall be in a fair way, when the Isthmus Canal is open, to reap an abundant harvest. The disingenuous menacing attitude and diplomacy of some of the European powers will not do for us nor keep alive the spark of friendship, nor warm the Siamese heart towards the United States, but rather tend to make them fear and shun us.[43]

Smith believed that the best way to maintain friendly relations with the Siamese was to avoid the pitfalls of the European colonial empires. Thus he recommended that the United States extend its commercial influence without actual territorial gain. This eventually became the principle upon which the Open Door Policy was based. In time, Barrett incorporated Smith's ideas into his own world view and contributed to the climate of opinion among American policy makers which brought about the issuance of the Open Door Policy.[44]

2. All are Tributary to King Commerce—The Mood of the Northwest, 1884–1898

THE mood of the Northwest in the 1880's and 1890's was one of excitement and expectation over the future growth of the United States. Commercial expansion was an integral part of this growth process. Washington and Oregon commercial interests cultivated public opinion in their behalf with a thorough publicity campaign in regional newspapers and trade journals. They not only called for the expansion of foreign markets for their own native industries, but tied this to the development of a healthy national economy as well. Their political spokesmen in Congress were successful in gaining the necessary appropriations to develop the port facilities of Puget Sound and the Columbia River. This important government action made possible an expanded volume of exports for sectional and national commercial interests.

The most pressing reason given by businessmen and their publicists for expanding foreign markets was to meet the challenge of international commercial competition. In advocating this cause, men of commerce sought to enlist the aid of the government of the United States. This was considered necessary to combat the programs of government aid in foreign states. Because of the policies of these countries, especially of Germany and Great Britain, commercial expansion and foreign policy had become intimately connected. For the United States to compete effectively, Washington would have to accept commercial expansion as a component of foreign policy.

The underlying factor that sent this international commercial race into high gear was the progress of industrial and technological developments among the advanced nations. With the production capacities of these nations at such high levels, foreign markets were thought to be necessary to rid their economies of surpluses and keep them healthy.

To a greater and greater degree in the decade of the 1890's, the government of the United States considered American commercial expansion within the realm of foreign policy.[1] The acquisition of the Philippines, the announcement of the Open Door Policy in China, and the consequent commercial and political involvement of the United States in the Far East established this policy as fact. The period prior to these events witnessed an organized effort on the parts of Northwestern businessmen and politicians to bring the United States into the Pacific commercial arena. An understanding of this milieu in which John Barrett matured as a young adult is essential to an understanding of his later career as a publicist and diplomat.

Although the early settlers of the Pacific Northwest were the first to propose to Congress that harbor and river improvements be undertaken at Puget Sound and along the Columbia River to promote the expansion of commerce, it was not until the construction of the two transcontinental railways in the Northwest in the 1880's—the Northern Pacific and the Great Northern—that a well organized effort was made to influence Congressional legislation to benefit Northwestern commercial interests. With the transcontinental railways providing links between the Atlantic coast and Northwestern ports, the next logical step was to develop these ports and establish steamship lines to continue the "highways of progress" across the Pacific to Asia and southward to Latin America. To this end, both the Northern Pacific and the Great Northern railways established steamship companies to export the surplus products of the Northwest, and also the

South and Midwest via their railways, to markets in Asia and Latin America.

In 1893 the Tacoma *Daily Ledger* published a speech by George B. Dodwell of the Northern Pacific Railroad and Steamship Company.[2] In this speech, Dodwell explained how, in 1884, the Northern Pacific had sent a commission to China and Japan to inquire about expanding American markets in the Far East. As a result of intense competition from the nationally subsidized Canadian Pacific Line, the Northern Pacific had to expand its service to meet the challenge. In order to do this profitably, new markets had to be found to encourage a greater volume of exports. The Far East was believed to offer the best possibilities.

In this same speech Dodwell also recounted the strategy of the Northern Pacific Company. The company had called upon the government of the United States to support trade expansion so that American commerce would have a strong incentive to compete for world markets. Spokesmen for the company had argued that this would not only provide for sectional and national economic growth, but serve as an extension of American foreign policy and enhance the position of the United States in the eyes of foreign powers.

A campaign was then launched in the newspapers of the Northwest to win government and public support for commercial expansion. The image of a great inland China trade with a potential of 400,000,000 consumers was paraded before the public eye. The China market was ripe for the commerce of the West. What was needed now was government support through such things as ship subsidies and direct leadership in the quest for economic expansion.[3] In addition to the national accrual of wealth that would result from government aid, it was argued that the competition among west coast cities for these new foreign markets would be the life-blood of American progress.[4]

The Northern Pacific's program resulted in positive achievements. In direct response to the suggestions of the Northern Pacific Company, the Tacoma Chamber of Commerce had been organized in 1884. In addition, Washington and Oregon congressional representatives soon embarked upon a campaign to have the national government develop port facilities on Puget Sound in Washington and the Columbia River transportation facilities in Oregon.

The *Congressional Record* contains a number of proposals introduced by these men in the 48th Congress (1883–1885).[5] Specific measures included the designation of Tacoma and Seattle as ports of delivery, and the building of bridges, wharves, and docks to enhance their commercial capacities. Though Washington did not become a state until 1889, these were the first proposals for developing major port facilities there.

Other proposed legislation relating to Oregon called for the extension of the limits of the port of Portland, and appropriations for the construction of canals and locks at the dangerous Cascades on the Columbia River. This was needed in order to make the hinterlands of Oregon accessible to the large-scale river traffic developing around Portland.

Each congress after the 48th Congress contained its standard quota of bills for the development of Puget Sound. They were often introduced at the requests of boards of trade and private corporations. In the 51st Congress (1889–1890), Washington Senator John B. Allen, a friend of the Northern Pacific Company,[6] introduced proposals to develop Puget Sound, Gray's Harbor, and Olympia Harbor, to establish a naval station at Puget Sound, and to provide government subsidies for steamship lines.[7] In the 52nd Congress, Congressman William H. Crain presented a report on the advisability of a government-owned ship canal to connect Lake Union with Puget Sound in order to create a fresh water harbor.[8]

In 1893, the year in which the revelations of the Northern Pacific Company were published in Tacoma, another episode was unfolding in the story of Northwestern commercial expansion. In Everett, Washington's Bay View Hotel, James J. Hill, president of the Great Northern Railway, the chief rival of the Northern Pacific, told an audience of businessmen:

> Your timber interests are your greatest source of wealth. . . . Your principal foreign trade will be with Japan. We are ambitious enough

to put on a line of fast-going ships from our western terminal to run to Japan.[9]

Hill had great hopes for developing an extensive commerce with the Far East not only in timber but in cotton, steel, and flour.[10] He envisioned a vast railway network associating all sections of the United States in a mammoth exchange of commerce. The surplus products of the North, South, East, and West were to be collected in the ports of the Pacific Northwest and shipped to the Orient.

With the completion of the Great Northern Railway to Everett, Washington in 1893, and the installation of a steamship line to Japan, James J. Hill could have asked for nothing better than for the development of Everett Harbor. As if at Hill's behest, Senator Watson C. Squire of Washington introduced a bill in Congress (1894) to inquire about the dredging of the sand bar at Everett in order to make a fresh water harbor near the Snohomish River.[11]

A fresh water harbor was preferable to a salt water harbor for a number of reasons. Timber constructions would be permanent in fresh water and logs and wooden boats could be stored indefinitely. Iron-hulled ships could benefit from the opportunity to have corrosive salts removed in fresh water. In addition, there would be no tidal variations, and a large number of ships could be anchored in this protected port.[12]

Schuyler Duryee of the Everett Land Company wrote to Secretary of War Daniel S. Lamont that the "proposed improvement would be of great commercial benefit to Everett in view of its many industries."[13] As a consequence of this, he called upon the national government to lay harbor lines from Puget Sound to the Snohomish River for the benefit of the Great Northern Railway and Steamship Company, and the growing commerce that was being drawn to Everett.[14] In response to such petitions, Congress approved the Squire Bill. The improved harbor facilities were completed in the next five years.

In marshalling material in support of the development of Everett Harbor, Senator Squire employed information conveyed to him by the Reverend Alexander Alison.[15] The Reverend Alison was a world traveler and publicist for the commercial prospects of the Pacific coast. It was quite common for businessmen and politicians to employ the arguments of such publicists in order to strengthen their own positions, and thus succeed in passing their proposals. Fred Harvey Harrington's study of another churchman and commercial publicist, Dr. Horace Allen, American Minister to Korea from 1897 to 1905, further documented the role played by such men in American commercial expansion.[16] Charles Denby Sr., American Minister to China from 1885 to 1898, and Julean Arnold, Consul-General in Peking, were also familiar with the work of churchmen and missionaries as "pioneers of commerce" and agents of progress.[17]

While Washington state businessmen and politicians worked hard to improve port facilities and expand export markets, Oregon leaders too were engaged in like enterprises. The Columbia River was to Oregon and the cities of Portland and Astoria what Puget Sound was to Washington and the cities of Tacoma, Seattle, Olympia, and Everett. Astoria, at the mouth of the Columbia, envisioned itself as a future west coast New York City, and Portland, farther up river, as another Albany.[18] Portland leaders, however, considered the city to be in a position similar to Paris, and Astoria as LeHavre. But regardless of their viewpoints, both cities worked to develop their ports and the river. The very existence of this competition insured agitation for expanded commercial enterprise.

In the 42nd Congress (1871–1873), Oregon Congressman James Slater introduced the first bill for the improvement of Columbia River facilities, and Senator H. W. Corbett proposed a ship-building subsidy to promote exports.[19] Slater argued for the removal of obstructions to navigation on the Columbia and Willamette rivers to aid the commercial growth of Portland. The city's chief commercial liability was the difficulty of maintaining an adequate channel to the sea, which was over a hundred miles away. The depth of the channel averaged about ten feet. At the mouth of the Columbia, where Astoria was situated, was a sand bar over which the depth was only twenty feet. Large ships could not go above Astoria.[20] Goods were shipped primarily by barge and rail from Portland to

Astoria. Fear of competition from Puget Sound ports, however, drove the people of Oregon to request aid from the national government. After a series of petitions, Congress approved a bill in 1883 providing for the removal of the sand bar, and the deepening of the channel by the joint efforts of the city of Portland and the national government.[21]

Each congress after the 42nd Congress had its share of similar bills. Such requests came from Portland and Astoria merchants, municipal boards of trade and private corporations. In 1880, the Ladd and Tilton Bank petitioned Senator James Slater to request $750,000 from Congress for a breakwater at the mouth of the Columbia River.[22] Within the next decade the breakwater was built by the national government, and Astoria petitioned to become a major port of entry.[23]

Harbor and river developments, however, were not the only concerns of Oregon and Washington commercial interests. The *Congressional Record* was filled with the supplications of their representatives. In 1880 Oregon Senator James Slater called for a canal at the Isthmus of Darien (Panama) to serve world commerce, and promote the industry and international trade of the Columbia River and Puget Sound regions.[24] In the following session of Congress, Oregon Senator LaFayette Grover proposed that the canal be built in Nicaragua.[25] Proposals for one or the other location were made in succeeding congresses. Petitions were presented in behalf of the Puget Sound Lumber Manufacturers, the Oregon Patrons of Husbandry, and the Seattle Lumber Manufacturers Association.[26] Clearly the northwestern lumber industry was in a favorable position to increase its trade with the construction of an interoceanic canal. The Trans-Mississippi Commercial Congress, meeting in 1892, looked upon the construction of the canal as a great step in the commercial evolution of the Pacific coast.[27]

The laying of a Pacific telegraph cable across the Ocean to Asia was another primary objective of Northwestern businessmen and politicians. Speaking in 1895, Senator John Mitchell of Oregon expressed the views of the Northwest:

Senator Mitchell. I believe that the commercial, naval and political necessities of the United States require not only that a submarine telegraph cable shall be laid between the western coast of the United States and the Sandwich Islands, but I believe that such a cable should be extended by way of Samoa to New Zealand, Australia, and on to Japan. I have long believed this to be true and I took action in the Senate looking to the construction of such a cable nearly five years ago.

Senator George Gray (Delaware). Does the Senator think that the relations between that group of islands in the Pacific Ocean and the United States are sufficient of itself to justify the expenditure of $3,000,000 by the United States Government?

Senator Mitchell. I certainly do think so. I think the line in itself would be of great commercial and political advantage to the people of the United States, even if it were not extended any further.[28]

It was not the mere existence of the harbors that made great commercial cities on the coast, but the interactions and communications among men of commerce the world over. A trans-Pacific cable was indispensable for such men.

Until a cable could be established, however, newspaper and trade journal articles served as a principal means of publicizing commercial opportunities. Promises of economic growth were never lacking. The major newspapers of the Pacific Northwest carried an abundance of "boom" articles endorsing the expansion of markets into Asia and Latin America.[29] Especially noteworthy contributions came from American diplomatic representatives. *La Revue Diplomatique,* the organ of the French Diplomatic and Consular Service, made particular note of this:

> The Americans are practical men, and their instinct for business is marvelous. Nothing is more characteristic in this respect than the organization of their consular corps. . . . It is recruited principally from journalists, who carry into their official careers the trained instinct of observation, the quick grasp of passing events which belong to their former profession. They remain in close sympathetic touch with their former readers. . . . The American consul does not understand that he has a commercial situation to maintain, but always a commercial situation to conquer. His ingenuity is exercised to investigate and find new markets.[30]

Although journalistic experience was helpful to commercial publicizing in the diplomatic corps, it was not essential. Certainly the lack of such training did not keep American officials from reporting commercial opportunities to Pacific coast business interests. The American Consul in Brazil, J. Dockery, wrote in the Seattle *Post-Intelligencer* that the Latin American market was eager for American products.[31] He advised the American business community to meet its responsibility, or forever rank behind the British and other foreign merchants. Furthermore, he suggested that commercial expansion had been a very useful tool for the extension of foreign policy in other countries. The United States could learn from this.

Similar articles appeared in other papers. United States Consul-General at Shanghai, William Leonard, wrote in the San Francisco *Chronicle* that the China market was just waiting for American manufacturers, and that he was pleased to see that American industries were responding.[32] W. D. Tillotson, American Consul at Kanagawa, Japan, pointed to the American potential in Japanese markets in an article in the Tacoma *Daily Ledger*.[33] In addition he implored American consuls everywhere to do everything they could to aid American merchants in the quest for new markets. This was thought to be the only way to take markets away from the British and other European industrial powers. The Portland *Morning Oregonian* carried articles and editorials of the same nature.[34] Within a short time, John Barrett himself would be fulfilling a similar role from his posts in Siam and Latin America.[35]

American consuls and Northwestern newspapers were not the only ones supporting trade expansion. Speaking before the Tacoma Chamber of Commerce in 1894, Secretary of the Navy Hilary A. Herbert told his audience:

> Your future looks toward China, Japan, and the rest of the East. If you are to become great in commerce that is the way you must look. . . . You will reach not only to China and Japan but to Russia with her teeming millions of population to buy from you. . . . It is a fact well established that our own people are not yet aware of the possibilities of the Asiatic trade.[36]

Tacoma businessmen already looked forward to the day when a

steamship line would be established between Tacoma and Vladivostok.[37] From Vladivostok the United States could then tap the internal markets of Russia by shipping over rail and along the Amur River. These businessmen believed that a great market existed for American dry goods, iron, machinery, coal, farm tools, lumber, and cotton.[38] In order to reach these markets, former Governor Gilpin of Colorado had proposed at one time a plan to build a railway from Seattle to St. Petersburg by way of the Behring Strait.[39] This particular scheme may have been impractical to most businessmen, but the market it envisioned was quite real to them. Men of commerce believed that in their lifetimes the star of empire would find its destiny westward across the Pacific.[40]

In an editorial supporting the admission of Chinese merchants to the city of Tacoma, the *Daily Ledger* summed up the position of Oregon and Washington commercial interests:

> Our great markets must necessarily be to the South and West of us. We must trade with the millions in the vast empires that lie toward the setting sun, who want our flour, wheat, timber, coal, and other manufactured and natural products. Unless we do this we shall be left far behind in the race for commercial supremacy. . . . Unless we advance we must inevitably retrograde. . . . It is a critical period, a turning point in our history.[41]

A number of trade journals held a similar interest in the expansion of commerce. The *Northwestern Miller* founded the Millers' League of the United States in 1887 whose aim, among other things, was to expand American flour exports.[42] The *Pacific Lumber Trade Journal* had long advocated the expansion of markets to the Pacific, Europe, Latin America, and Africa.[43]

The *Northwestern Lumberman* called upon the government of the United States to embark upon a complete program of aid to private industry for the purpose of expanding markets. In an 1897 editorial entitled "The German Way," the journal outlined the pattern of government aid to business in Germany.[44] Under a policy of government protectionism, German manufacturing interests had developed to a point from which they could challenge international markets. The government then stepped in to develop foreign trade by granting subsidies, bounties, tax benefits, and establishing a corps of commercial agents in foreign countries to study carefully local market situations. The *Lumberman* believed that a similar policy should have been followed by the United States, but was afraid that the government considered it too paternalistic.[45]

The influence of German thought on aspects of American progressivism has been carefully explored.[46] This influence extended not only to American scholars, but in time to members of the American business community who admired the policy of government regulation and leadership to promote greater industrial efficiency.[47] But even before this position became popular among businessmen, Senator Albert J. Beveridge of Indiana in 1892 had praised Germany's scientific appraoch to government administration and its relation to foreign commercial expansion.[48]

Some twenty years later, advisers to Woodrow Wilson continued to propound similar ideas. Secretary of Commerce William C. Redfield in *The New Industrial Day* spoke of commerce as an ally of progress.[49] He said that this was especially true in relation to foreign trade: "Our domestic business needs to feel the throbbing pulse of the larger world of foreign commerce. 'One must be done, the other not left undone!' Stability in home markets depends largely on ability in foreign ones." [50] Germany had set an example in this respect which Redfield felt the United States had to follow.[51] Efficiency in production and organization were the keynotes.

Another of President Wilson's advisers, Charles Ferguson, a special commercial representative to the American business community, sought to promote commerce through the development of a more scientific spirit within business organizations.[52] To Ferguson, the general problem of uplifting the standard of living and mobilizing society's creative forces could best be solved by the insights of engineering—by the efficient organization and use of resources and production.[53] This approach included the fostering of market expansion as Germany had done.

Arguing in a similar manner as Redfield and Ferguson, Edward

N. Hurley, Shipping Commissioner of the War Industries Board, also praised the German government's interest in the progress and promotion of commerce, and recommended that the United States proceed along similar lines:

> If we wish to avail ourselves of the great trade opportunities which exist today in foreign markets, the business organization of our foreign competitors is an eloquent argument for cooperation [under the aegis of the national government] in America's export trade. . . .
>
> The development of American foreign trade is not only a privilege, but a duty of American businessmen. It is a field in which the national wealth and prestige can be increased.[54]

As a result of the wartime experience of the United States, the Wilson Administration moved toward the realization of these policy recommendations. The systematic marshalling of economic power was further expanded as a result of the rivalry between the United States and Japan in the Far East. This led to the renewed participation of the United States in the international banking consortium in China in 1918, and the passage of the Webb-Pomerene Act which permitted American corporations to cooperate in the pursuit of foreign commerce without fear of anti-trust prosecution. The government of the United States had now become a leader in the field of foreign commercial expansion. And there was little in the way of debates as those which plagued the McKinley, Roosevelt, and Taft Administrations with regard to the proper role of the national government in sponsoring and directing commercial progress and expansion into foreign markets. The policies of the national government would in fact be accelerated in the 1920's under the tutelage of Herbert Hoover as Secretary of Commerce and then as President.

From the trend of later developments, the *Northwestern Lumberman* had indeed shown great insight into the impact of commerce and industrialism on the role of the Government in fostering economic progress. The journal continued to print articles and editorials that further defined how the United States might achieve the success that Germany had won. In an article by Theodore Search, president of the National Association of Manufacturers, a five-point program was offered as the basis for the development of new markets in Latin America and the Far East.[55] Search called specifically for (1) the holding of international expositions, (2) world-wide reciprocity agreements, (3) consular reform, (4) the establishment of a government department of commerce and manufacture, and (5) restoration of the American merchant marine.

International expositions and world's fairs provided a medium to acquaint prospective buyers with a nation's manufactured goods. In addition such regional meetings as the Trans-Mississippi Exposition, which was to meet in Omaha in 1898, afforded the opportunity for manufacturers to come together and discuss methods of achieving greater efficiency in the production of their goods, and ways to expand their markets at home and abroad.

As far as reciprocity was concerned, Search advocated that the tariff be removed completely from politics. He called for a tariff based on economic considerations alone. International trade was a vital interest to the United States. A tariff policy of high protectionism put into effect at the behest of certain vested interests could not be expected to facilitate the marketing of American products overseas. Search argued that what the United States needed was a flexible policy of selective reciprocity. In this way those industries which needed protection for their domestic markets could have it, and those which sought commercial expansion through foreign trade could have that. Neither industrial group would have to sacrifice itself to the interests of the other.

Search's position on consular reform resulted as a direct consequence of the policy of the McKinley Administration.[56] When McKinley took office in 1896 he initiated major changes in ninety-eight of one-hundred and fifty consulates to pay off Republican patronage debts. Search charged that

> No business institution could survive such demoralization as this, and it is not reasonable to expect that so essentially commercial an institution as the consular service can be disorganized at will without impairment of efficiency.[57]

To combat similar occurrences with each change of administration, he suggested that certain changes should be made in the Consular Service: (1) there should be as few changes in personnel as possible, (2) removals should be made only because of demonstrated incapacities, (3) vacancies should be filled by promotions and transfers, not through party patronage, (4) appointments and promotions should be made by merit, and (5) only American citizens should be appointed to consular service.[58]

The establishment of a Cabinet-level department of commerce and manufacture had been a major aim of the National Association of Manufacturers for a long time.[59] Search argued that the progress of industrialism in the United States had made it necessary. The prosperity of the manufacturer could almost be equated to the prosperity of the nation. The National Association of Manufacturers called for the new department of commerce and manufacture with the incorporation of such bureaus as the Geological Survey, the Bureau of Rivers and Harbors, and even the Consular Service itself. In this way greater total efficiency and coordination could be achieved in the production and distribution of goods in domestic and foreign markets. The arguments of the National Association of Manufacturers were influential; for in February, 1903, President Theodore Roosevelt created the Department of Commerce and Labor.[60]

The final item in Search's program was the restoration of the American merchant marine. This was crucial if the United States was to have its share of foreign trade. The rapidly expanding foreign trade of the United States heightened Search's awareness of the decline of the American merchant marine. As Search noted, "American manufacturers no longer measure their productive capacity by the consuming power of their home market; for the world is their market and all people of the earth are their customers." [61] The United States could not depend forever on subsidized foreign shipping to transport its ever-expanding volume of trade.[62] The economic challenge that the United States had made to the other industrial powers could not be effectively carried out as long as the United States used the shipping facilities of competitors to try to win markets from them. To meet American commercial needs, Search called upon the Government to subsidize the merchant marine:

> . . . it is the unquestioned duty of a modern government to provide for the quick and direct transport of the mails. . . . Further than this, it is the general function of a government to arrange for the national defense, and naval subventions . . . are not unusual in aid of lines which agree to build their vessels in such a way that they may be readily converted into transports or cruisers in time of war. Some governments have gone still farther than this, and have held that the opening up of new transportation routes upon the sea will bring so much economic benefit to a country . . . that the subventions are made . . . solely upon this account.[63]

The *Northwestern Lumberman* agreed wholeheartedly with these measures, and lent its editorial voice in support of their adoption. It called for the establishment of a tariff commission to take the tariff issue out of politics and establish rates on a sound scientific economic basis.[64] It also praised international trade expositions such as the Philadelphia Commercial Museum, which had been established on a permanent basis, and suggested the establishment of similar organizations.[65]

The journal was adamant in its call for consular reform. It stated that professionals in various industries should be named as consuls and commercial attachés because only a man with a thorough knowledge of an industry could look after its best interests. Naturally the lumber industry was number one on its list. If lumbermen were appointed consuls, it was argued, they could work to foster new markets and add to the efficiency of production by making the evaluation of markets more accurate.[66] In addition, an increase in lumber exports would give work to railroads and other carriers, and stimulate other businesses. Idle American labor would be put to work, and a richer and healthier society would result as the finished product.[67]

In order to implement properly these changes, the *Northwestern Lumberman* was in favor of lessening the role of politics in governmental administration. It called for a single eight-year presidential term because "A general election and change of administration every four years are a great damage to the business and industrial interests of the country, and a serious hindrance to the progress and prosperity of the nation." [68] With a guaranteed eight-year presidency, political appointments would be decreased, and professionals, once appointed, would be more likely to accomplish their tasks without interference. This last suggestion entailing a change in the nature of governmental administration from a political base to a professional base represented the epitome of progressive reform; that is, a scientific approach to the problems of government in an industrial society.[69]

Between 1884 and 1898 one underlying motive for American commercial expansion in the Pacific Northwest was a natural outgrowth of American industrial society. The American economy had come of age so that it was now in a position to challenge other industrial powers. The basic desire for economic gain on the parts of private enterprises in the Northwest was the most evident cause of overseas commercial expansion for their particular interests. But the Northwest as a geographical unit was caught up in the complexity of American industrial society, and therefore followed a national as well as a regional trend toward commercial expansion.

In their quest to compete for foreign markets, Oregon and Washington commercial interests were able to secure the support of the national government to develop the transportation facilities of Puget Sound and the Columbia River. The direct influence of businessmen upon the government of the United States to further economic gains was clear. As in the cases of the Northern Pacific and Great Northern Railway and Steamship Companies, their spokesmen initiated publicity campaigns which eventually led to legislation favorable to their special commercial interests, and to the promotion of commerce in the Pacific Northwest.

It is noteworthy that these campaigns for commercial expansion in the Northwest were underway well before the infamous depression of 1893. Recent interpretations have pointed to this depression as a catalyst for American trade expansion into Asia and Latin America. One historian has written:

This consensus [of political and business leaders] resulted from the depression which struck the United States from 1893 to 1897. During these years concise and conscious economic analyses by the Cleveland Administration, the business community, and the leading congressional figures led these three groups to conclude that foreign markets were necessary for the prosperity and tranquility of the United States.[70]

Such an observation, although correct, does not explain the purposeful movement to promote overseas expansion of Northwestern commerce in the 1880's and 1890's prior to the depression of 1893.

Similarly, another scholar has said that "The Panic of 1893 and the 'awakening of China'—economic need and apparent opportunity—these were the propellants of America's expansion across the Pacific." [71] It is true that both economic need and apparent opportunity were the propellants for American commercial expansion, but these motives existed in the Northwest long before the depression of 1893.

The commercial expansion of this section evolved in part with the completion of the transcontinental railroads and the industrial development of the Northwest. Plans were underway for the installation of steamship lines across the Pacific, and for Oregon and Washington harbor and river developments years before 1893. Foreign markets were considered necessary in the Northwest for the prosperity of the region and the entire United States *before* the impact of the depression of 1893 made this fact plain to the Cleveland Administration and to the rest of the country. With the impact of the depression, however, a new national push for export markets was undertaken.

A clue as to why historians have emphasized this new surge for commercial expansion after the depression of 1893 may be found in a significant article on the causes of the depression.[72] This study observed that American export expansion had only been *arrested* during the depression.[73] Thus the depression had temporarily halted the expansion of markets which were already in the process of development. The renewed expansion after the depression appeared to be in direct response to it rather than a return to previous growth patterns. The purposeful expansion of Northwestern commercial interests in the 1880's and 1890's provides an excellent example of these growth patterns.

Another motive that was put forth in the Northwest for commercial expansion was the argument that it aided directly in the extension of American foreign policy in Latin America and the Far East. This position appeared noticeably in the diplomatic corps. Indeed the life of John Barrett provides ample evidence of it. The newspapers of the Northwest were well aware that a race for commercial supremacy existed among the industrial nations. This was why the reports of diplomatic officials were so often published with favorable editorial comments. The government of the United States, however, had lagged behind in recognizing and acting upon the full impact of this race for commercial empire.

It was not until the acquisition of the Philippines, and the annunciation of the Open Door Notes of 1899 and 1900 that the United States officially began to challenge European economic and political supremacy in Asia and Latin America on a grand scale. In effect, the United States said to the other industrial nations, "We will bury you economically."

This is not to say that the exclusive causation factor in American diplomacy was economic. This motive did exist and was very powerful. But to the commercial interests and politicians of the Pacific Northwest economic concerns bore directly upon governmental policies in both domestic and foreign matters. The role assigned to the national government in fostering foreign exports, and the methods that were suggested were clear evidence of it. In this milieu John Barrett matured as an exponent of commercial expansion.

3. With John Barrett
in Asia and Latin America,
1894–1906

IN the years 1894 to 1906 John Barrett served in a number of excellent positions to make use of the education he received in the Pacific Northwest as a commercial publicist. While Minister to Siam (1894–1898) he used his authority to call upon commercial interests in the United States and State Department officials alike to heed his arguments for a concerted effort to expand American foreign trade in Asia. Following his term in Siam, Barrett approvingly observed the growth of the United States into a full-fledged imperial power as a war correspondent with Admiral Dewey in the Philippines. With these broad experiences, Barrett was just the man the Republican Party's Speakers Bureau wanted to publicize America's commercial opportunity in the Far East under the Open Door Policy to chambers of commerce and trade associations from coast to coast. In like manner, Barrett was a natural choice to serve as commissioner-general in the Far East for the St. Louis World's Fair in 1904.

Barrett's career as a commercial publicist was a success, but he preferred to return to the diplomatic service. Although he hoped for an assignment in the Far East as minister to China or Japan, State Department rivalries and political patronage thwarted his plans. Faced with these obstacles, he shifted his field of activity to Latin

America. From 1904 to 1906 he served in a succession of ministries in Argentina, Panama, and Colombia. By 1906 his reputation as a commercial publicist and diplomat was so enhanced that the new Secretary of State Elihu Root chose him as Director General of the reorganized Bureau of American Republics. In this capacity John Barrett would receive his greatest recognition as an exponent of commercial expansion.

From his diplomatic post in Siam, John Barrett continued his work as a major advocate of expanding American participation in Asian affairs. Imperial competition among the western powers had been a longstanding threat to American expansion in Siam—and indeed all Asia. In a significant communique to Secretary of State Walter Q. Gresham, Barrett warned of the threat to Siamese autonomy posed by British, French, and German gunboats.[1] Because of the great tension among the colonial empires, three immediate dangers existed: (1) France could annex Siam to Cambodia in order to halt British expansion beyond Burma, (2) Britain might try to add Siam to Burma as a means of outflanking the French, (3) Germany could call for the division of Siam into spheres of influence in its strategy to catch up in the race for empire in the Far East.

Barrett argued that since Siam's wealth and resources were of central interest to the oriental trade of the United States, an American show of force was necessary to preserve its position in Siam. Barrett also suggested that the Siamese Ministry itself would welcome an exhibition of American power in order to blunt the thrust of European influences. As bulwarks to American involvement in Siam, he appealed to the State Department for American gunboats, and a well publicized government endorsement of increased American commercial expansion in the Far East.[2] Barrett was not a traditional territorial imperialist in calling for this forceful action. Rather, he hoped to preserve the integrity of Siam and equality of commercial opportunity there. He had no designs upon the territory of Siam as such; it was Siam's commerce that he wished to safeguard for American interests. Secretary of State Gresham, however, refused to send one gunboat without some immediate issue to justify such a move.[3] Although temporarily thwarted, Barrett soon was able to achieve his objective of increasing American power in Asia through diplomacy; namely, through his handling of the little-known Cheek Teak Wood Case.[4]

The case involved an American medical missionary and concession hunter, Dr. Marion A. Cheek, who was advanced 600,000 ticals by the Siamese Government to be used in the working of the teak forests near Chengmai, and for the purchase of teak wood. When Dr. Cheek failed to maintain the interest payments on his loan, the Siamese Government claimed default. It seized his timber as payment on the basis that Dr. Cheek, having violated his contract, lost his right to the property. Thus the original owner, the Siamese Government, reclaimed its property.

In the resulting lawsuit Dr. Cheek claimed that the Siamese Government confiscated property without due course of international law, and in violation of the treaty rights of the United States in Siam providing for extraterritoriality. The case was ultimately submitted to international arbitration under British Chief Justice and Consul-General at Shanghai, Sir Nicholas J. Hannen, and decided in favor of the United States.

The significance of the Cheek Case was that the decision upheld the prestige of the United States as a major western power in Siam in particular and in Asia in general. It specifically kept British, French, and German interests from gaining favor in Siam at the expense of an American set back. In addition, Barrett was able to get the show of force he wanted as a result of an incident growing out of the decision.

On November 16, 1896, Minister Barrett sent United States vice-consul E. Vernon Kellett and his aide to look after the Cheek estate at Chiengmai.[5] Siamese troops assaulted and arrested Kellett for this action. Barrett immediately protested to the Siamese Foreign Minister, Prince Devawongse, and called upon the State Department to send a gunboat to protect American lives and property. This indeed was cause for alarm. The United States gunboat *Machias* was despatched from China and arrived at Bangkok in February, 1897. Kellett was freed when the United States threatened to use force to bring about his release. The Siamese Government subsequently appologized and there were no further incidents. Although the retiring Secretary of State, Richard Olney, thought Barrett over-reacted, the newly appointed Republican Secretary John Sherman acknowledged with approval Barrett's handling of the incident.[6] The following November, the Kellett assault case was decided in favor of the United States, and the western oriented Siam *Free Press* claimed a victory for Minister Barrett and American diplomacy.[7]

Although Barrett enhanced his reputation by his handling of the Cheek Case, his greatest long-term accomplishments came as an exponent of commercial expansion. Repeatedly he urged the State Department to compete with European powers for export markets in the Far East. The rate of growth of American Asiatic trade was too slow in relation to the potential markets. When Lawrence E. Bennett, an American civil engineer, received the concession to install electric lighting in Bangkok, Barrett took the occasion to lecture the State Department on the inadequacy of its policies:

> Had American companies or American interests made earlier and stronger efforts, in accordance with repeated previous reports and recommendations of mine, other concessions and other opportunities for the development of commerce, trade, and general business could have been secured and seized, which have gone into the hands of companies and representatives from European countries. . . .
>
> Finally, as suggested by Mr. Bennett's concession, I would urge through the Department of State, what I have said many times before, that now is the time for American material interests in the Far East to be built up from Japan to Java. One of the greatest opportunities in the world is here. Great Britain, Germany, and France are competing more hotly everyday for the chief share of [Siam's] growing business and trade. Their merchants, exporters, steamship companies, and commercial representatives are leaving no stone unturned to thoroughly exploit the fields open in Japan, China, Siam, and neighboring lands and colonies. May America awake to the situation before it is too late.[8]

This was a prominent theme in all of Barrett's writings. In a key article in the *North American Review*, Barrett said, in effect, that the best way for the United States to expand its overseas interests was to undertake further commercial extensions without actual territorial gain.[9] This principle upon which the Open Door notes were based was espoused by Barrett three years before Secretary of State John Hay issued the first of his famous notes in September, 1899. This is not to say that Barrett was directly responsible for the Open Door policy. Barrett did represent, however, that climate of opinion on the nature of American expansion which led to the adoption of the Open Door principles.[10]

The essence of the Open Door Policy was to tap the economic wealth of China—and all of Asia for that matter—without assuming the political and military responsibilities that normally accompanied territorial acquisition. To this end, the United States called upon the competing powers in China to accept the principle of equality of commercial opportunity (September, 1899), and to guarantee the territorial integrity of China (July, 1900). In this way the United States could overcome competitive spheres of influence by making all of China accessible to American trade.

In addition to this suggestion which eventually became part of the Open Door Policy, Barrett closed his article with a plea for increasing the efficiency of legations and consulates, and the establishment of a corps of commercial attaches to aid businessmen seeking foreign markets. This was deemed the best way to "Awaken interest in the hunt for the Golden Fleece of Cathay." [11]

Barrett's role as a publicist for commercial expansion was highly praised. Oregon Congressman Binger Hermann warmly thanked him for supporting the expansion of American exports,[12] and Charles H. Dodd, president of the Portland, Oregon Chamber of Commerce, told Barrett that his letters encouraging trade expansion were circulated among Oregon and Washington businessmen.[13] Theodore Search, president of the National Association of Manufacturers, wrote to Barrett that "I have read with much interest your recent extended report on the foreign trade of Siam and I think that the information you have given ought to be of much value to all those who are interested in the extension of the foreign trade of the United

States." [14] Search also requested the names of business houses in Siam that would be prepared to cooperate with the National Association of Manufacturers in handling more American products.

Barrett also received a number of direct communications from American businessmen and corporations interested in the markets of Siam. These included letters from the United States Export Association of New York, the Monarch Bicycle Company of San Francisco, Chicago, and Toronto, the Export Printing and Publishing Company, the Hammond Typewriter Company, Gould's Manufacturing Company of New York, the Marion (Ohio) Steam Shovel Company, the Wolff, Sayer, and Heller Sausage Company of Chicago, and the Empire Moulding Works of New York (which confided to Barrett that they were "indebted to the United States Consuls for [their] success" in foreign markets).[15]

A number of trade inquiries were received from west coast interests as well. These included requests for market information from the Spencer-Clarke Import Company of Portland, the Wolff and Zwicker Iron Works of Portland, the San Francisco Bureau of Foreign Commerce, Closset and Devers Spice Importers of Portland and Lovett M. Wood, editor of the *Trade Register* (Seattle).[16]

Barrett's promotion of west coast commerce was so welcome to Oregon Congressman Binger Hermann that he spoke to Robert R. Hitt, Chairman of the House Committee on Foreign Relations, about finding a way to enlarge Barrett's duties and salary as Minister to Siam.[17] Barrett received a letter from Chairman Hitt in which Hitt told him that Barrett's plan to build up the merchant marine was most practical, and was "recognized and adopted in the St. Louis Platform" of the Republican National Convention in 1896.[18] This was a rare tribute since Barrett was still nominally a Democrat.

As much as Hitt agreed with Barrett's suggestions, he believed that some of them were beyond the scope of government. In particular he thought this way about the idea to recruit commercial attaches from mercantile houses for duty in the State Department. By 1920, however, the role of the national government had so expanded under progressive leadership that commercial attaches were a reality. Under the direction of Warren Harding's Secretary of Commerce, Herbert Hoover, commercial attaches were regularly sent to American embassies for the purpose of expanding American export markets.

Similar views on the scope of government were held by Senator Stephen M. White, a member of the Committee on Commerce.[19] He admired Barrett's proposals, but he did not think that the government had the power to carry out all of them. On the issue of expanding foreign trade, however, he was in total agreement with Barrett, and believed that the United States had not paid attention to the opportunities that were available.

Congressional support of this nature was vital to Barrett. But for him to be effective as a publicist his own position had to command a certain amount of prestige and authority. Given this condition, 1896 emerged as a critical year. Barrett found it impossible to support the Democratic candidacy of William Jennings Bryan in the Presidential election beyond a modest financial contribution.[20]

Although Bryan's silver policies might result in a boom in Asiatic trade because silver was Asia's standard of currency, Barrett was not prepared to see the United States gamble on a soft money policy. Debased currency such as inflated silver would undermine the benefits of any new trade agreements in the long run by lowering the value of the dollar in international exchange. Barrett simply could not support this position.

Historically the adoption of the gold standard in Great Britain (1821), Germany, and France (1870's) coincided with the expansion of foreign markets. In order to maintain confidence in the value of the dollar, the United States would have to employ a monetary system in accord with the other principal industrial trading nations. To depart from this economic theory and adopt silver or bimetallism would allow the European nations to capitalize on the monetary weakness of the United States.

Silverites and bimetallists thought differently. A combined gold and silver standard would give the United States a competitive edge in the Far East and Latin America where the silver standard was dominant. They argued that the United States should concentrate on trade with the underdeveloped areas without unnecessary regard for European policies. This would create a competitive advantage for expanding American markets. Both gold supporters and silver and bimetal advocates favored commercial expansion. Disagreement came over the means of gaining the best benefits.

Barrett, however, believed that the prosperity of the United States had been built upon a sound gold dollar, and this should continue to be its standard. Thus after McKinley's victory, Barrett wondered what the President-elect's policy would be toward men like himself; that is, Democrats driven into Republican ranks by Bryan's silver policy.[21]

Since diplomatic appointments were primarily a matter of special political patronage, Barrett was replaced by a Republican, Hamilton King of Michigan. Barrett, however, did remain as Minister to Siam until 1898 in order to complete the Cheek Teak Wood Case.

Despite his removal for reasons of political patronage, his work in Siam was praised. Secretary of State Sherman had commended him for his handling of the Kellett affair.[22] The Bangkok *Times Weekly Mail* called him the leading American authority on Southeast Asia.[23] At his farewell dinner Dr. Hays, chairman of the Bangkok Tramways Company, said of Barrett:

> As regards our commercial interests we feel that Mr. Barrett's able reports to our Government as well as correspondence with chambers of commerce and contributions to various journals will be no small factor in arousing our country's interest in the trade with Siam and the Far East.[24]

John Barrett was not as yet fated to leave the Far East. While he was stopping over in Hong Kong, the War with Spain erupted. Barrett was offered the opportunity to become a special war correspondent for the William Randolph Hearst syndicate. He quickly accepted the position, and was assigned to Admiral Dewey's flagship.[25] This offered him the opportunity to witness first-hand America's military thrust toward empire.

From his war experience Barrett wrote a book entitled *Admiral George Dewey*. In it he related Dewey's views on the war and the acquisition of the Philippines. It was evident that the war gave Dewey the opportunity he had long awaited. Prior to his Pacific appointment he had said to a friend:

> I am approaching rapidly the years of retirement and will soon be out of it all with nothing to my credit but gradual and honorable promotion. I do not want war, but without it there is little opportunity for a naval man to distinguish himself.[26]

In the light of this statement one can only conclude that Dewey did welcome war with Spain. Furthermore, as a spokesman for American interests in the Philippines, Dewey became an enthusiast for American empire:

> I have great expectations for the future of the Philippines. I hope to see America's possessions the key to oriental commerce and civilization. The brains and money of our great country will develop the untold agricultural and mineral richness of the islands. We shall never sell them. Such an action will bring on another war. We will never part with the Philippines, I am sure, and in future years the idea that anybody should have seriously suggested it will be one of the curiosities of history. Our moral responsibility to the natives and the world will not allow us to retreat from what is before us.[27]

The war performed wonders for Barrett as well as for Dewey. Barrett embarked upon a world tour to publicize the "great expectations" of an optimistic America at the dawn of a new century of peace and commercial growth under American leadership. In accordance with this theme he set about the task of writing articles and making speeches and appearances before prominent commercial and political organizations. He was hired by the Republican Party's Speakers Bureau for $140 a week in 1900 to publicize American commercial potential in Asia and the Pacific.[28]

In remarks he prepared on the nature of imperialism, Barrett made plain his support of the American version of empire:

> Before Dewey's victory, the United States was regarded everywhere in Asia by the common people and by the governing classes as a secondary power. Our commerce and our influence were hampered and checkmated. The glorious achievement of May 1, 1898, and the subsequent occupation of the Philippine Islands make America actually respected and treated as a first-class power for the first time in the history of our relations with Asiatic nations.

> We would have been laggards instead of leaders in rescuing our minister and missionaries at Peking [during the Boxer Rebellion], and we would have been the last instead of the first power to have led in the protection of life, property and rights in China, if we had not held, by moral as well as material right, our new position in the Philippines. If eight millions Filipinos do not yet understand us, eight hundred millions of other Asiatics have been taught to respect our flag and country for all time.[29]

Barrett viewed the position of the United States in the Philippines as one that presented a direct challenge to British hegemony in Asia. In a London speech before members of the British House of Commons, Barrett said that he expected Manila to rival Hong Kong and Singapore as a great commercial and naval port.[30] He pointed to the example set in Newchuang, Manchuria where the United States had increased its share of Manchuria's total trade from 15 per cent to 60 per cent. This he attributed to "the persistent agitation for American commercial opportunities by American ministers and consuls." [31]

Barrett also expressed a fear of Russian influence in Manchuria to his British audience. He suggested a union of British, American, Japanese, and perhaps German efforts in a coordinated China policy to combat the Russian threat. Since the interests of the United States and Great Britain extended throughout China, Barrett welcomed British support of what was to be the Open Door principles of equality of commercial opportunity and territorial integrity as a means of maintaining access to all China. Thus the virtual division of China into spheres of influence would be checked:

> Russia with Manchuria on the North, Germany with Shantung, and France with the territory contiguous to her dominions on the South, are naturally largely satisfied by what would come to them in a division of territory, and unless *Great Britain and the United States, whose interests extend all over China,* assert themselves there will be no powerful direct influence to preserve the integrity of that Empire.[32]

In awakening the United States to its opportunities, Barrett could not help boasting about the role that diplomats and publicists such as himself had played. In a significant article, "The Paramount Power of the Pacific," in the *North American Review* he stated his feelings about his role:

> Ever since I first went to the Far East, inspired with the belief that the western coast states of America must look to the Pacific for the development of permanent conditions of prosperity, I have been a devoted advocate of the American opportunity in the Pacific. For five years I have hammered away in reports to the Government, letters to chambers of commerce, and contributions to newspapers, magazines, and reviews including particularly the *North American Review,* with the hope of thus awakening our Government, as well as our manufacturers and exporters, to an appreciation of the splendid field awaiting their best efforts.[33]

His work was now beginning to bear fruit at last. Unfortunately it took a major depression and a war to impress upon the American government and business community that this great opportunity in the Pacific was quite real.

This article was actually more important, however, for Barrett's views on a viable future China policy for the United States. The China market was more than a myth to John Barrett, and he presented arguments to prove its potential:

> China and other Asiatic countries want all the flour and timber, and a goodly portion of other kinds of food and raw products which California, Oregon, Washington, and neighboring western states can supply; they want the manufactured cotton and raw cotton of the South in increasing quantities, and the time may come when the Pacific Asiatic demand will take up the surplus supply of the South's great staple; they want the manufactured cotton, iron, steel, and miscellaneous products of the North and East, together with the unlimited quantities of petroleum; they want corresponding manufactured products of the Central West, and there is no reason why there should not be developed among the Asiatic millions a demand for the Central West's great staple, maize (or Indian meal), such as there has been created for flour. . . .[34]
>
> China possesses unlimited quantities of coal and iron, which are already located; and there are numerous indications of gold and silver and other precious metals. There is no valid reason why China should not be covered with a network of railways. She has the population and the products to support them. *It is often contended that China can never be a great commercial nation as has been predicted by many authorities because she has not the buying capacity. There is no better way to develop*

such capacity than by opening up the interior. Money will flow in
from the outside to purchase raw supplies, and will provide the people
with means to buy the manufactured products of other nations.[35]

When we consider that the cotton mills of New England and the
South are supplying this demand in Manchuria, and that they have been
kept running when other mills have been closed, there is every reason
why those two sections should join together in insisting that the open
door shall always apply to Manchuria.[36]

Barrett's arguments were based upon the belief that China would
remain in a colonial position for many years to come. China was
to be a never ending market for American manufactured goods.
Essentially, this depended upon the construction of an internal
Chinese railway system to tap the buying power of the population.
In this way the Chinese could purchase large quantities of manufactured goods from the West with the income they received from the
sale of raw products.[37]

It is questionable whether or not this buying power really existed,
or could have been developed in sufficient volume to sustain the
amount of trade envisioned.[38] Barrett, however, was certain in his
own mind that these markets were real and would be fully exploited.
His faith in the power of the free enterprise system, and the progress
of industrial nations was all-consuming. A new century was about
to begin, and the United States was in the vanguard of the civilized
world. For those with faith all things were possible. John Barrett
was a man of deep faith in American progress.

In order to safeguard a role in the progressive development of
China for the United States, China had to be protected from dismem-
berment. To this end, Barrett proposed a six-point program:

A reasonable and logical conclusion as to our present policy in China
could be summarized as follows. First, we should stand firmly and persist-
ently for the integrity of the Chinese empire, and use our influence
for the inauguration of reforms of government; second, we should insist
on the 'open door' and absolute freedom of trade, in accordance with
the stipulations of the old Tientsin treaties, from Canton to New-Chwang;
third, we should direct our political and moral influence against the
delimitation of alleged 'spheres of influence,' or actual 'areas of operation,'
and withhold formal recognition thereof until, or unless, fourth, seeing

the inevitable development of such spheres and the consequent break-up of the empire—without willingness to resort to war—we should demand and insist upon the open door and freedom of trade *with* and *in* these areas of *quasi* sovereignty; fifth, we should consider the advisability of securing a port in northern China, but only in the event of the break up of the empire, or by legitimate purchase and treaty; and sixth, the United States as far as possible should work in harmony and on the same lines with other powers having similar commercial interest, to protect them from further limitation.[39]

Above all John Barrett wished to maintain the political integrity of, and freedom of access to, China. But if this became impossible he was prepared to suggest alternative policies including guarantees of freedom of trade *within spheres of influence,* and the acquisition of a port city by the United States. One should not consider the proffering of these alternatives, however, as evidence of Barrett's willingness to acquiesce in a reversal of the traditional policy of the United States in China.[40] The Open Door approach to China was always the keystone of Barrett's policy proposals.

Barrett not only addressed himself to the large American industrial and agricultural interests concerning the China market, and to political policy makers, but to workingmen in the cities and on the farms as well:

> The masses of our people, especially the laboring classes, are inclined to think that the Chinese question is one which should not concern them, and in the haziness of their view they may think that it has to do with Chinese labor, which, of course, looms up to them as a mighty danger, while in fact they are as much concerned as the manufacturers and exporters, and are today in many sections of the country and in numerous establishments absolutely dependent upon the Chinese market for their employment. The farmers of the West and South can unite with the laboring men of the North and East in supporting the shippers and manufacturers and exporters in developing a strong Asiatic policy. Were the door of China closed against us tomorrow, it would mean that labor and capital alike would suffer immeasurable harm. They should therefore see that it is never closed.[41]

To Barrett's mind foreign markets would serve as outlets for surplus products and social tensions between capital and labor. Thus he carried Frederick Jackson Turner's frontier thesis to the shores of Asia. There was no doubt in his mind that the development of Chinese markets would be a positive good for the United States.

Speaking before the New York Chamber of Commerce in June, 1899, Barrett pointed to the United States as the sole arbiter of China's future.[42] All the powers in China had declared spheres of influence for themselves except the United States. In fact the United States did not have a treaty or agreement with the controlling powers regarding freedom of trade. Barrett counseled that the United States should find a way to maintain its freedom of trade and China's territorial integrity as well. He spoke these sentiments three months before the first Open Door note concerning free access of trade in China was issued by Secretary of State John Hay in September, 1899. It was not until July, 1900 that the State Department issued the second Open Door note pertaining to the territorial sovereignty of China.

In the same speech Barrett said that it was up to private American commercial interests to arouse and educate the public sentiment so that the Government would be confident of support in promoting American foreign commerce.[43] In his concluding remarks he said:

> There is no need of talking of war or showing force, we can accomplish our results without such drastic steps and methods. Firmness in supporting our treaty rights, with public sentiment awake to our present and possible interest in China will accomplish the desired result.[44]

This plea was echoed a few months later before the American Asiatic Association of which Barrett was an honorary member.[45]

These statements clearly expressed the need for a policy of American commitment in Asia. Force was not the answer. This had been Europe's stumbling block in its colonial relations. The United States could achieve better results through the unity of commercial and governmental policies supported by public sentiment. Barrett believed that in this way the United States would gain commercial influence without the military and political liabilities that were concomitant with traditional colonial expansion.[46] The Open Door Policy was the embodiment of this rationale. With the realization of this policy, Barrett was certain that the United States had fought its last war in Asia.[47]

John Barrett did not simply view the American presence in Asia in commercial terms alone. It was more accurately part of the expansive progression of American civilization. American civilization was not only a business civilization, but a Christian civilization. Eventually the two concepts became fused together. In an address entitled "The Future of Missions in Asia from a Layman's Standpoint," Barrett tied the endeavors of churches and chambers of commerce together in advancing American interests.[48] Speaking of missionaries, he said that they were helpful in preparing the way for commercial expansion, and that they invariably preceded the merchant in penetrating the interior of Asia. They were a necessity to the Asiatic statesman and his people because they provided them with the knowledge needed to undertake genuine progress and development.[49] Their mission was to bring civilization to the Asiatics—a business civilization.

Barrett was pleased that the McKinley Administration had taken steps toward the goals Barrett himself had outlined. With the Presidential campaign of 1900 fast approaching, Barrett supported William McKinley for reelection.[50] Continuing his work to enlist support for the expansion of American empire for the Republican Party's Speakers Bureau, Barrett portrayed the Philippines as the "Antilles of the Orient," and rejoiced at the prospect of a determined policy toward China. Barrett endorsed the Open Door Policy (McKinley Doctrine) in Asia as a necessary complement to the Monroe Doctrine in the Western Hemisphere.

> We have a Monroe Doctrine in America; shall we not have a McKinley Doctrine in Asia? . . . Commerce is the life-blood of nations. The commerce of Asia may yet be needed to give us the strength to conserve the governments and commerce of the Americas. The McKinley Doctrine in the Pacific and China may provide the sinews of war to defend the Monroe Doctrine in the Americas.[51]

Once again echoing Frederick Jackson Turner's frontier thesis,

Barrett saw the policy of the McKinley Administration in the Pacific as the natural culmination of western progress:

> America's present position in the Pacific which today commands the attention of all nations and stands sponsor for the first great political issues of the twentieth century, would seem, in the light of history, to be the logical conclusion of a long line of succeeding events and the legitimate consummation of imperious world movements.[52]

These "imperious world movements" were the expansions of European powers along the western frontier. The United States was heir to these developments, and from the beginning was "set toward the Pacific." [53]

The driving force behind this expansion came as a result of the progress of Western man. In the case of the United States, Barrett also noted a "A desire to benefit their own [American] interests, . . . mingled with a sense of neighborly help, which showed itself in dealing with Japan, China, Korea, and Siam." [54] The Open Door Policy was considered by Barrett as part of a chain of treaties extending from the first tea trade with China in 1784, through the trade agreements with Siam and China in the 1830's and 1840's, and down through the Tientsin (1859) and Burlingame (1869) Treaties with China.[55]

In the contemporary link of this chain of tradition, Barrett personified Japan as the natural partner of the United States in Asia.[56] He did not suggest a formal alliance with Japan, but believed that as a result of common purpose on the parts of both nations, "they could call a halt to the movements of any nation, or they could refuse to heed the restrictions of countries which might meddle where Japanese and American interests should be supreme." [57]

As a result of his prowess as a publicist for Asian markets, Barrett received a number of endorsements for the post of Commercial Commissioner for Asia. He had long desired to return to the Far East in a diplomatic capacity. Commercial Commissioner was not exactly what he wanted for himself, but it would place him in a position to move into a major post. He received the support of such diverse interests as the North Carolina Bankers' Association, B. I.

Wheeler, president of the University of California, the Missionary Society of the Methodist Church, James T. Law & Company, the Commission Merchants of Cincinnati, the Engineers Club of New York, and Charles R. Flint, author of *The Open Door from an Industrial Point of View.*[58]

Despite their efforts, Barrett was not appointed to the commission at this time, although he became commissioner-general for Asia for the Louisiana Purchase Exposition in 1902–1903. In the meantime he continued working for the Speakers Bureau. His chief aim was to expound the potentialities of the China market to a larger circle of commercial interests, and to the public in order to gain broad support for the Open Door Policy.

Speaking before the National Association of Merchants and Travelers, February 5, 1901, he stated:

> The best experts agree that the Chinese are by nature born merchants, and if given an equal opportunity with other countries, under the protection of a progressive government and with the interior of the mighty empire open to the world, would surpass the remarkable record of Japan during the last thirty years. . . . America has only begun to exert herself in the competition for Asian markets.[59]

In 1900 American trade with China amounted to $45 millions. Barrett expected to see it rise to $450 millions once the interior parts of China were tapped. He suggested that the United States begin importing heavily from China to help pay for return shipments on American vessels, and to increase American railroad traffic from the coast to the interior of the United States.[60] Barrett concluded:

> in the new Pacific, in the new Asia, and in the new China to come, we shall make our influence supreme if we construct the trans-Isthmian canal, buy the trans-Pacific cable, and build up together our navies of commerce and war.[61]

In an article in *Harper's Weekly* (April, 1901), Barrett pointed to the importance of Manchuria in the American trade picture.[62] The United States was selling more manufactured goods there than in any other province of China. But the commercial expansion of the United States was meeting fierce competition from Russian commercial and political expansion. Russia had made inroads into the American market for cotton goods, flour, and petroleum. At the very time Barrett was writing this article, the Russians were planning a policy of harassment against the American "colony" in Newchwang, Manchuria.[63]

Despite such competition, Barrett did everything in his power to show that investment in China was safe. Not only did he publicize the Open Door Policy as evidence of the government's resolve to support American business ventures, but he drew a parallel between the development of American and Chinese cultures:

> The fact that the Chinese were not indigenous adds vastly to interest in the study of the growth of the empire. It established a degree of sympathy, on our part, with their history that we might not otherwise feel. [Just as the Americans drove the Indians before them] so the Chinese, entering their new field of effort, gradually drove before them the natives until now there are left only small numbers of aborigines. . . . The Chinese seem to have begun their empire with isolated bands of colonists in the northern, central and western provinces of Shensi, Shansi, Honan, and Hupeh, just as the first Europeans established themselves in Massachusetts, Virginia, and Florida.[64]

Barrett wanted to prove China a nation of progress and civilization from its earliest evolution. He argued that this tradition coupled with the aid of progressive American policies guaranteed the future success of China as a modern nation.

In the face of Barrett's widespread publicity and acceptance, a campaign was launched to have him appointed as minister to China in the spring of 1901. The Portland, Oregon Chamber of Commerce and Board of Trade wrote to Oregon senators John Mitchell and Joseph Simon that they strongly supported Barrett's candidacy.[65] The chambers of commerce of San Francisco, Los Angeles, Dallas, Texas, Nashville, Tennessee, Sacramento, Tacoma and Seattle endorsed him to President McKinley.[66] Senator Mitchell wrote to the President:

> Mr. Barrett has the support of nearly every commercial and trade organization on the Pacific coast, as also that of many of the most influential and leading businessmen of the Pacific coast states, and also a strong

and influential support from leading businessmen from many of the Eastern and Middle states. . . . I feel confident his efforts would result in promoting to a very great degree our commercial interests.[67]

Senator Redfield Proctor of Vermont said that Barrett's knowledge of commercial conditions in Asia made him a great value to the United States.[68] He also had the endorsements of Congressman H. G. Foster of Washington, Senator J. B. Elkins, Robert R. Hitt, Chairman of the House Committee on Foreign Affairs, and Charles Grosvenor, Chairman of the House Committee on Merchant Marine and Fisheries.[69]

In addition private business firms wrote to the President praising Barrett's work. These included the Charles Nelson Lumber Company of San Francisco, the Sperry Flour Company of San Francisco, G.B.M. Harvey of Harper and Bros. Publishers, the well known commercial publicist and engineer Daniel A. Tompkins of the Southern Manufac- turers Club, the Merchants Association of New York, and the South- ern California Fruit Exchange.[70] F. B. Thurber, president of the United States Export Association, thought that Barrett's appointment would greatly strengthen the McKinley Administration's policies in the Far East.[71] The Board of Foreign Missions of the Presbyterian Church believed that John Barrett would enhance the general prestige of the United States in the Far East.[72]

At this time, however, the vacancy that Barrett expected in China did not materialize. The incumbent Minister to China, Edwin H. Conger, decided not to retire. But even if there had been an opening in China, there were certain individuals in the State Department and in the diplomatic corps in the Far East who opposed Barrett's appointment. Secretary of State John Hay preferred William Wood- ville Rockhill for the post, as did Theodore Roosevelt.[73] But the real leader of the faction in opposition to Barrett was Francis M. Huntington-Wilson, head of the American Legation in Tokyo and later Chief of the Far Eastern Division of the State Department (1905–1909), and Undersecretary of State (1909–1913).[74] Within a year, Barrett would discover this "conspiracy" against him.

Barrett was given an appointment, however, as an American

delegate to the Second Pan American Conference in Mexico City (October, 1901 to January, 1902). The Conference was suggested by President McKinley to continue the operation of the Union of American Republics and Commercial Bureau, and to confirm American friendship toward Latin America after the war with Spain. The instructions given by President Theodore Roosevelt, who became President after McKinley's assassination in September, 1901, to the American delegation further defined the purpose of the Conference:

> The chief interest of the United States in relation to the other republics upon the American continent is the safety and permanence of the political system which underlies their and our existence as nations—the system of free self-government by the people. . . . It should therefore be the effort of this commission to impress upon the representatives of our sister republics . . . that we desire, above all, their material prosperity and their political security, and that we entertain toward them no sentiments but those of friendship and fraternity.
>
> It is not therefore opportune for the delegates of the United States to assume the part of leadership in the conference. . . . Great care should be taken not to wound sensibilities . . . or to take sides upon issues between them. . . . Conciliation should be continued . . . throughout the conference and every effort made to secure the greatest possible unity of action. . . .
>
> It will be prudent to propose nothing radical, to favor a free expression of views among the delegates of the other powers, and to favor and support only such measures as have the weight of general acceptance and clearly tend to promote the Common Good.[75]

There were also secret instructions by Roosevelt against the institutionalization of compulsory arbitration in hemispheric matters.[76] The United States was prepared to accept arbitration on a voluntary basis, and according to agreement among the immediate parties involved. The important thing was that the United States was not to have its freedom of action restricted by a formal multilateral dictate from the Latin American republics. Despite this disposition, compulsory arbitration was adopted by Argentina, Bolivia, the Dominican Republic, Guatemala, El Salvador, Mexico, Paraguay, Peru, and Uruguay, but the United States refused to be a party to it.[77]

Barrett's role at the Conference was a minor one. He did serve on the reorganization committee of the Bureau of American Republics. This was rather prophetic for in 1907 he would be chosen Director-General of the Bureau. In this capacity Barrett helped to fulfill some of the longstanding goals of the Bureau's founder, and the man whose ideas had exerted such a strong influence on him in his earlier life, James G. Blaine.

But at the time of the Conference, Barrett was more interested in returning to the Far East than toiling in the Latin American field. He soon received his wish. As a result of his reputation as a commercial publicist, and the wide support he commanded, he was selected to serve as Commissioner-General for Asia for the Louisiana Purchase Exposition to be held in St. Louis in 1904. This was made to order for Barrett for the scope of the Fair embraced all the facets of American progressive leadership on the one hundredth anniversary of the purchase of Louisiana from France.[78]

Exhibitions from over thirty nations and every state in the Union exemplified modern developments in the arts, industry, manufacturing, agriculture, mining, forestry conservation, and technology. The exchange of international trade and broad concepts regarding the nature of international cooperation were prime goals of the Exposition. John Barrett had the difficult task of persuading the nations of the Orient to participate.

He traveled extensively, addressing various chambers of commerce in the nations of the Far East. He met with Wu Ting Fang, former Chinese Minister to the United States and a commercial publicist in his own right, and Japanese Foreign Minister Takahira, and gained their support and participation. Although he found a great deal of apathy and ignorance regarding the purpose of expositions, he was able to convince China, Japan, Ceylon, East India, Siam, and New Zealand to participate.[79] For this contribution, exposition officials and diplomats alike praised his work.[80]

Speaking before a group of businessmen in Portland, Oregon Barrett emphasized the importance of the exposition:

At St. Louis for the first time in our new commercial and political association with the Orient, the Trans-Mississippi states which have been looking out so eagerly on the Pacific, will see the real and actual resources and possibilities of Asia and her exact capacity for demand and supply. They will then understand the significance of President [James J.] Hill's efforts to secure cheap land and water transportation, and the necessity of low freight rates to stand the competition of European subsidized steamship lines and Siberian government railways. . . . You can form some idea of what the World's Fair means to the Trans-Mississippi section as a grand opportunity of acquiring and exchanging information for the mutual benefit of Asia and America. . . .

Let us pull together, for then we can the sooner realize Seward's magnificent prophecy that the Pacific will become the theater of events surpassing in its worldwide influence the Atlantic and the countries bordering thereon.[81]

Although his work for the Exposition was important to Barrett, his personal goal was to regain a diplomatic post in Asia. In this pursuit he was undercut, once again, by party politics. While on his Asian tour for the Exposition, he received a wire from Secretary of State John Hay offering him the post of Minister to Japan.[82] The former minister, Alfred Buck, had died suddenly. Barrett was ready to accept the offer, but he received another telegram from Hay instructing him to decline the position.[83] The reason given was that the Japanese Government considered him *persona non grata* because Barrett's home state, Oregon, championed Japanese immigration restrictions.[84]

In reality it was Mark Hanna who had objected to Barrett's appointment.[85] Alfred Buck had been his appointee, and he was not ready to surrender the important patronage post of Minister to Japan. Hanna chose Lloyd C. Griscom, the son of the shipping trust magnate and Hanna's close friend Clement Griscom, as Minister. Thus the system of party patronage again thwarted the thrust of Barrett's ambition.

Barrett found this hard to accept. He was convinced that someone had eliminated his candidacy through stealth. Many older diplomats were jealous of his too rapid rise to success and the great deal of publicity he received. Barrett believed that Francis M. Huntington-Wilson, chief of the Tokyo Legation, had been primarily responsible.[86] Barrett said that Huntington-Wilson wanted the post for himself, and so made the Japanese Government believe that the United States Legation in Tokyo had not been in favor of his appointment.[87]

Barrett and Huntington-Wilson also held conflicting views on the Asian policy of the United States. Barrett believed that the United States could work best with Japan in achieving its objectives in Asia because both nations were progressive.[88] Huntington-Wilson considered this interpretation a mistake. He instead favored stronger cooperation between the United States and Russia to offset Japanese opportunism.[89] Huntington-Wilson saw Japan as a greater long-run threat to the United States in Asia than Russia. Whereas Barrett envisioned an informal alliance between the United States and Japan (a position close to that of President Theodore Roosevelt's), Huntington-Wilson saw Japan as a singularly expansive power bent upon its own ambitions.

The Russo-Japanese War of 1905 threw an even bigger scare into Huntington-Wilson.[90] As early as February, 1901, Barrett had predicted this war and the victory of Japan.[91] Russia was corrupt and reactionary. It had to give way to modern, progressive Japan. This position, however, became increasingly unpopular in the diplomatic corps of the United States in the Far East as Japan showed signs of resisting the role of "footman" for the Open Door Policy of the United States in China. The honesty of the Japanese in their informal partnership with the United States to preserve China's integrity had come under suspicion. To be sure, Japan had designs of its own in Asia that were in direct opposition to American policies.

Barrett, however, still believed that it was to the benefit of both Japan and the United States to develop the resources and markets of a progressive China together because of the advanced state of progress in both American and Japanese societies. Quite naturally, Barrett was terribly disappointed with the turn of events, but he still hoped for an appointment in the Far East. In lieu of the Japanese post, however, President Roosevelt made him Minister to Argentina with the intention of later promoting him "in accordance with the wishes of the Pacific coast." [92]

From 1903 to 1906, Barrett served as Minister to Argentina, Panama, and Colombia in succession. As a determined exponent of commercial expansion, he used these posts as stepping stones to a position that carried real authority. He originally hoped to return to the Far East, but he was well aware that the Latin American field offered as much promise to American economic growth as did the Far East. Thus he mapped out a new strategy for a commanding post in Latin America.

He made his wishes known quite early by filing formal applications for appointments either as Ambassador to Mexico or Director-General of the Bureau of American Republics.[93] But it was two years more before he was appointed to head the newly reorganized Bureau of American Republics. In the meantime he continued his work as a publicist for foreign markets. He wrote to President Roosevelt that Latin American markets were full of great promise.[94] He called for the inauguration of a "new era" in American relations with the nations to the South in order to combat European influences there. His concrete suggestions included reciprocal trade agreements, the expansion of mail and passenger ship lines, American branch banks and corporation offices, the production of goods specifically for the Latin American market, and the sending of commercial agents to Latin America.[95]

Barrett believed that the key to this "new era" should be the Bureau of American Republics. In this way the United States could cultivate closer relations with Latin America and especially its nearest neighbor, Mexico. Barrett, of course, had his eyes set on both the Directorship of the Bureau and the Ambassadorship of Mexico, and hoped to lead the way personally to the "new era" of progress in Latin America.

Barrett's appointment to Argentina had been widely acclaimed. Albert Shaw's *Review of Reviews* noted:

Mr. Barrett's training eminently qualifies him for servicing American interests where there is real work to be done; and the only two fields of foreign service which could at this time well interest a man of his temperament and energy are in the Orient and South America.[96]

Munsey's Magazine pointed out that the selection of John Barrett was especially

> interesting in view of the general desire among Americans for better relations with their sister republics and the President's known intention to raise the standard of diplomatic appointments to South America.[97]

National Magazine saw the Barrett appointment as a step in the right direction:

> The plan of the United States government to raise the standard of our official representation in South and Central American countries—a project inaugurated by the appointment of John Barrett as minister to the Argentine Republic, is another move in the shrewd game which Uncle Sam is playing, in the hope of carrying off the prize for which all the progressive nations of the world are now striving, namely the trade of South America. . . . Mr. Barrett is admirably adapted for such work. . . . In short, he is a diplomatic promoter of the first class.[98]

Although Barrett had been thwarted in his quest for a diplomatic post in the Far East, he did have the respect of the Roosevelt Administration. This assured him the opportunity for success in Latin America. But Argentina was not the place to achieve that goal. Thus he requested a transfer to a more "active" post.[99]

In 1904 Barrett was appointed Minister to Panama after serving only a few months in Argentina. In his new capacity he contributed to the mediation between the Panamanian Government of President Amador, and the United States Canal Commission.[100] The problem centered around the fact that the United States had established Ancon as a closed port and opened a United States Post Office in the Canal Zone. Both of these moves were a direct challenge to the national integrity of Panama. Barrett offered a solution to ease the tension that existed between President Amador and the Governor of the Canal Zone, General Davis. He proposed that Panamanian and American Canal Zone authorities communicate through his office to avoid face-to-face confrontation.[101] This solution was accepted and led to a successful conclusion of the difficulties. The air was cleared considerably by the fact that Barrett was able to produce a letter written by Philippe Bunau-Varilla in which the rights of the United States were clearly defined.

With the conclusion of this matter, Barrett used this opportunity to suggest that the American Legation in Panama be closed, and that the offices of American Minister and Governor of the Canal Zone be merged for more efficient service.[102] This suggestion caused quite a debate in Washington. President Roosevelt himself first agreed with the proposal and then changed his mind for fear that too much power might be placed into one man's hands.[103] But the Legation was closed, and Barrett was appointed Minister to Colombia.[104]

There were a number of reasons for this maneuver. First, the Bowen-Loomis scandal became public and necessitated the removal of Herbert Bowen from Caracas.[105] This meant a shift of personnel in the Caribbean. William Russell was sent from Bogota to Caracas; John Barrett was transferred to Bogota; and Charles Magoon was made the Minister to Panama and the Governor of the Canal Zone. Second, President Roosevelt and a number of people in Washington thought that Barrett had called too much attention to himself in Panama.[106] Barrett had offended Canal Zone officials by his suggestions, and appeared to be taking all the glory associated with the Canal project for himself. In addition, Barrett had again engaged in pompous self-advertisement in the press. This was especially true concerning his work in the settlement of the smoldering boundary dispute between Panama and Costa Rica over the claims of contesting American fruit companies for disputed territory.[107]

Finally, the ambitious Barrett wanted a more influential position in Latin American affairs, and so he himself pressed for a transfer.[108] He had been promoting himself in official and public circles, and in accordance with his policies of furthering American interest in Latin America, he established a scholarship fund for American college students studying the Spanish language and culture.[109] In 1905 Barrett's optimism about his promotion and the beginning of a new era in Latin American affairs was borne out with the appointment of Elihu Root as Secretary of State upon the death of John Hay. Root took a noticeable interest in Barrett and welcomed his appointment as Minister to Colombia. Through his personal style of diplomacy, Barrett did a great deal to ease tensions between Colombia and the United States over the issues surrounding the revolt in Panama.[110] Barrett's growing friendship with Rafael Reyes, Colombian President, restored Colombian confidence in the United States. Reyes was persuaded to withdraw his government's demand for an indemnity from the United States, and prepared the way for a treaty of friendship.[111] Both Theodore Roosevelt and Elihu Root were quite pleased with Barrett's accomplishments.[112]

In actuality there was a definite community of interests among Roosevelt, Root, and Barrett; for their joint policies were aimed at establishing order and stability in the republics of Latin America by making them strong economically and politically. This was necessary for the United States to make full use of the resources and export markets available in Latin America. Thus Secretary Root embarked upon a program of Pan Americanism not unlike that advocated earlier by James G. Blaine and John Barrett.

Speaking before the Trans-Mississippi Commercial Congress in Kansas City, Root acknowledged the work of his predecessor:

Twenty-five years ago, Mr. Blaine . . . undertook to inaugurate a new era of American relations which should supplement political sympathy by personal acquaintance, by the intercourse of expanding trade, and by mutual helpfulness. . . .

The policy which Mr. Blaine inaugurated has been continued; the Congress of the United States has approved it; subsequent presidents have followed it. . . . Mr. Blaine was in advance of his time.

Now, however, the time has come; both North and South America have grown up to Blaine's policy. The production, the trade, the capital, the enterprise of the United States have before them the opportunity to follow, and they are free to follow, the pathway marked out by the farsighted statesmanship of Blaine for the growth of America, North and South, in the peaceful prosperity of a mighty commerce.[113]

Shortly after becoming head of the State Department, Root received an interesting memorandum from John Barrett concerning the manner of approach that the State Department should take toward Latin America.[114] Barrett said that the United States had patronized her sister repubics with a "holier than thou" attitude. He called instead for warmer, and more equitable relationships. In this way the United States would win the support of Latin American diplomats for her Pan American policies. Barrett advised Root to

> give South America more credit for its actual progress in national and municipal government, in education, in literature, in science, and in solving social and economic problems, and in generally striving under adverse conditions to reach a higher standard of civilization.[115]

It is difficult to say to what degree Barrett's words influenced Root directly, but the Secretary employed a manner of diplomacy in tune with Barrett's suggestions. It is known that both Theodore Roosevelt and Elihu Root thought well of Barrett's work as a diplomat.[116]

As Minister to Colombia Barrett had worked in conjunction with Secretary Root. During Root's good will tour of Latin America in 1906, Barrett made a tour of his own that was timed to coincide with the Secretary's arrival in Bogota. He traveled a thousand miles by mule train on an incredible journey over the Andes Mountains through Colombia and Ecuador to manifest the commercial possibilities of the interior of the South American continent once a modern system of transportation was constructed.

Upon completing his grand tour, Secretary Root announced at Bogota that

> I have been much gratified during my visit to so many of the republics of South America to find universally the spirit of a new industrialism and commercial awakening, to find a new era of enterprize and prosperity dawning in the Southern continent.[117]

A few days later speaking before the Trans-Mississippi Commercial Congress in Kansas City, Root put forth a seven-point program that was very similar to the measures that John Barrett had espoused first in relation to Asia and then Latin America.[118]

Following Barrett's suggestions Root called for (1) American manufacturers to produce the goods that Latin Americans wanted, (2) the learning of the Spanish and Portuguese languages by American businessmen,[119] (3) American producers to arrange their credit systems with those prevailing in the country where they wished to sell, (4) branches of American banks in Latin America, (5) American diplomatic and commercial agents to treat Latins with mutual respect, (6) engineers and technical experts to be sent to Latin America to increase production and trade, and (7) the improvement of communications and transportation.[120] Philip Jessup, Root's biographer, described this program as evidence of the Secretary's "remarkable understanding" of the commercial development of North and South America.[121]

In addition to these measures, Root strongly endorsed the idea of Pan American conferences, and the reorganization of the Bureau of American Republics. The conferences and the Bureau were to serve as vehicles for the realization of his overall policy.

John Barrett had long coveted the post of Director-General of the Bureau of American Republics. He had asked Nicholas Murray Butler to speak to the President and the Secretary of State in his behalf.[122] The Secretary wrote to Butler that he had a very good opinion of Barrett, but that he could not make any changes in the Bureau at the moment.[123] The reason was that the Third Pan American Conference was being held at that time in Rio de Janeiro, and was in the process of reorganizing the Bureau.[124]

At this conference, the scope of the Bureau was enlarged beyond that of a commercial organization. It was given permanent power to aid in securing the ratification of resolutions and conventions adopted by the International American Conferences. Secretary Root fully explained American intentions:

I think that the work of the Bureau of American Republics, the existence of the International Union, and the holding of . . . conferences afford altogether the best means of breaking up the comparative isolation of this country from the other countries of America. . . .

Our relation with them has been largely a political relation, while, on the other hand, their racial ties . . . [and] investment of . . . European capital . . . have made the whole trend of South American trade and social relations . . . subsist with Europe rather than the United States. . . .

Just at this time, of course, the great increase of capital in the United States is on the threshold of seeking investment abroad. . . . I take it to be the proper function of Government to help create situations of friendly relations and good understanding, which will make it possible for capital to go. . . .

It seemed to me that I could not do any more useful work to the country for the promotion of American trade relations and at the same time for the promotion of these relations which tend to maintain peace and harmony than to foster and advance this tendency which finds its expression through the Union of American Republics and these successive conferences.[125]

But another important goal of the Conference was the completion of the Pan American Railway, which was designed to connect Argentina, Chile, and the United States. The reorganized Bureau was needed to help in securing this project. Secretary Root revealed American policy when he said:

The success of the enterprise [railway] is desireable not merely because of the great and profitable traffic which it will secure for the United States, and for all the countries along the line, contributing to the prosperity and wealth of all, but because it will contribute to the internal peace and order of every country. Nothing polices a country like a railroad. Nothing material so surely discourages revolution and unites a people as adequate railroad communication.[126]

This statement was an excellent example of the change in American strategy under Root's direction. Recent dealings between the United States and Latin America had consisted of "big stick" diplomacy and forceful, self-appointed police power. The United States had seized the Canal Zone, established protectorates over Panama and Cuba, and assumed customs control in the Dominican Republic.

In putting forth a policy which actually amounted to "dollar diplomacy", Elihu Root desired to remove the charges of Yankee imperialism from Pan American diplomacy. What better way to prevent periodic police intervention by the United States than to create order and stability through peaceful commercial enterprise. Root had adopted the strategy propounded by James G. Blaine. To help implement this strategy, he chose John Barrett as Director-General of the Bureau of American Republics in the fall of 1906.

In naming Barrett to the post of Director-General, Root told

Edward M. Hood of the Associated Press that Barrett had been chosen because of his energetic character, his experience in diplomacy, his acquaintance with business methods, and his personal tact.[127] These qualities, he assured Hood, would "galvanize" into fresh life the International Bureau of American Republics.

Immediately upon taking office in 1907, Barrett embarked upon a campaign to publicize the work of the Bureau, and to encourage American businessmen to expand their markets to Latin America. To accomplish this goal he wrote a series of articles which appeared in a variety of publications.

In an article entitled "The Land of Tomorrow" in *Munsey's Magazine*, Barrett told of the new one million dollars Pan American Union Building to be constructed in Washington, D.C. by 1909 with a $250,000 congressional appropriation, and a $750,000 gift from Andrew Carnegie.[128] With this convincing piece of evidence that the United States Government was about to embark on a serious program to expand trade in Latin America, Barrett went on to talk of the new industrial movement there. He spoke of a potential market that could absorb many billions of American dollars.[129] The resources and markets were there. All American businessmen had to do was to develop them.

In *The Bankers' Magazine*, Barrett welcomed inquiries from capitalists, investors, bankers, and businessmen regarding the opportunities for the establishment of branch banks in Latin American cities.[130] He also advocated industrial loans, railway construction, electric lighting plants, waterworks, harbor improvements, and the development of agricultural, timber, and mineral resources.

Articles of this nature appeared in *The Review of Reviews*,[131] *The World Today*,[132] and *Systems*.[133] Time and again Barrett reiterated the role of the Bureau of American Republics in the promotion of trade expansion in the far-reaching opportunities of the South American continent. The Bureau's modern and efficient service had established a scientific approach to commercial expansion. Files were kept of the official reports on economic conditions in each of the republics. Newspapers and trade journals were gathered from everywhere in Latin America. Duplicate reports of American consular officials pertaining to commerce were made available to businessmen. American commercial investors also received personal counseling on foreign investment prospects from Bureau staff members. In addition the Bureau prepared handbooks and pamphlets on each country, giving vital statistics on exports and imports, trade conditions, tariff rates, public improvements, industrial opportunities, new laws affecting commerce, transportation and communication facilities, mining concessions, studies of monetary systems, and immigration policies.[134]

Secretary of State Elihu Root had taken a deep interest in the Latin American policy of the United States, and especially in the workings of the Bureau of American Republics. His choice of John Barrett as Director-General provided the organization with a first-rate administrator and commercial publicist. But Barrett himself had a broader vision of the Bureau than the Secretary of State, and most other leaders in Washington.

4. Director General of the Pan American Union, 1907-1920

BEYOND the realm of commercial publicizing, John Barrett hoped to make the International Bureau of American Republics, or the Pan American Union as it was known after 1910, a viable institution in hemispheric diplomacy. To this end he worked to define an active *political* role for the Union in such matters as (1) the creation of a multilateral approach to hemispheric affairs, (2) the Mexican Revolution, (3) the Pan Americanization of the Monroe Doctrine, (4) the uses of scientific knowledge and conservation studies for social progress, (5) the marshalling of the resources of Latin America in the World War effort, and (6) a plan to make the Pan American Union into a hemispheric league of nations.

In each of these issues Barrett hoped to expand the traditional commercial role of the Union into the political and diplomatic spheres. In this way he hoped to make the Union an instrument of social, economic and political stability and progress as James G. Blaine, the organization's founder, had originally planned.

During his first term as Secretary of State in the Garfield Administration, Blaine had set two objectives for American foreign policy in Latin America. The first goal was to bring about lasting peace in the western hemisphere. The second goal was to enhance commercial relations among all the American republics. In order to accomplish these aims, Blaine proposed in 1881 the establishment of a Peace Congress of American States to be held the following year.[1]

The Secretary had feared that the existence of war among the republics of Peru, Chile, and Bolivia would lead to European interference with the Monroe Doctrine.[2] European countries carried on a large volume of commerce with Latin America. It was in their interests that political stability exist to insure the smoothness of their operations. France in fact had proposed joint intervention with the United States to end the war, but the United States refused on the grounds that such action would modify the meaning of the Monroe Doctrine.[3]

If the United States had accepted the French offer to intervene jointly, the basic interpretation of the Monroe Doctrine would have been altered; that is, the United States would not have been able to claim its superiority in the western hemisphere over and above any European influence.[4] Blaine could not have allowed this to happen.

When the Monroe Doctrine was first announced unilaterally by the United States in 1823, it was done partly in opposition to British Prime Minister Canning's suggestion that the United States and Great Britain issue a joint declaration of protection for Spanish America against the Holy Alliance of France, Russia, and Austria. This unilateral maneuver allowed the United States to maintain its freedom of action in the western hemisphere.[5]

Again in 1852 Britain and France tried to influence the United States to issue a joint statement guaranteeing the neutrality of Cuba. Secretary of State Edward Everett refused their proposal because such a document would have gone against the principles of the Monroe Doctrine, and would have hindered American ambitions in Latin America. Thus in 1881, Blaine was following the traditional American policy of excluding European influence from the western hemisphere.[6]

Already the British Foreign Secretary, Lord Granville, had made it clear that Britain planned to hold the United States to the terms of the Clayton-Bulwer Treaty (April, 1850) which had provided for joint construction of any interoceanic canal. Faced with this situation, Blaine cautioned:

> If these tendencies are to be averted, if Spanish American friendship is to be regained, if the commercial empire that legitimately belongs to us is to be ours we must not lie idle and witness its transfer to others.[7]

In order to lessen European influence in Latin America and to promote American interests, Blaine proposed the creation of the Peace Congress of American States. The death of President Garfield, however, brought changes to the Cabinet that resulted in Blaine's removal as Secretary of State, and the cancellation of the Peace Congress. President Chester A. Arthur and the newly appointed Secretary of State Frederick Frelinghuysen were political antagonists of Blaine, and refused to listen to his plea to continue with his specific policies.

By 1883, however, the volume of European trade with Latin America had increased to such an extent that President Arthur sent three commercial commissioners to Latin America to discern what steps the United States should take to counteract this situation. They recommended that an inter-American conference be held to discuss commercial relations and arbitration procedures for the nations of the hemisphere.[8] Although the Cleveland Administration eventually opposed such a conference, Congress continued to support it.

Blaine had initiated the movement for a Pan American conference, but he was not primarily concerned with it during the years in which he was out of power, 1881–1889.[9] During these years, such men as Senators William McKinley of Ohio and John T. Morgan of Alabama, the commercial publicists Hinton Rowan Helper, former American Consul in Argentina, and William E. Curtis, the Northwestern newspaperman and future first Director of the Bureau of American Republics, continued to promote the Pan American movement.

In 1889, however, Blaine was again Secretary of State in the Benjamin Harrison Administration, and he endorsed the long-talked about plan for a Pan American conference to promote peace and commerce. He was especially optimistic for he felt that the United

States was now strong enough to challenge the favored position of European trade in Latin America. To this end, he planned to institute a series of reciprocity agreements with Latin America which would, in effect, bring about an American customs union patterned after the German Zollverein.[10]

The First International Conference of American States finally met in October, 1889, but Blaine did not succeed in his purpose.[11] The Latin American republics balked at a reciprocity system that gave new concessions to American industrial exports, but did not significantly alter the tariffs on Latin American raw materials. Blaine's reciprocity was looked upon simply as an attempt by the United States to seize European markets in Latin America.

Although Blaine's immediate plan was not realized he did succeed in the creation of the International Bureau of American Republics, and his Pan American policy, aimed at bringing about closer commercial and political ties with Latin America, eventually became a part of American foreign policy in the twentieth century.[12] David S. Muzzey, Blaine's biographer, has observed, as have other historians, that Blaine's Latin American policy helped to bring the Monroe Doctrine and Pan Americanism into harmony by paving the way for enlarging the unilateral scope of the Monroe Doctrine among the American republics. In time this resulted in mutual guarantees of peace and commerce. During the First and Second World Wars, the precedent of this Pan American policy helped to provide a rationale for the unified defense of the western hemisphere.

In moving toward a multilateral approach to hemispheric affairs John Barrett played a significant, though little recognized role during his tenure as Director-General of the Pan American Union (1907–1920). The first attempt that Barrett made to expand the diplomatic and political aspects of the Union along this line came as a result of the change in attitude toward Latin America during the Taft Administration. While Elihu Root was Secretary of State for the Roosevelt Administration, Barrett had been obviously pleased with the development of a policy of cooperation between the United

States and the republics of Latin America. Barrett's own influence on that policy was cause for self-satisfaction.

But with the advent of Philander C. Knox to the State Department, and the promotion of Francis M. Huntington-Wilson to First Assistant Secretary of State, Barrett felt that Root's policy and his own were in jeopardy. Despite the Taft Administration's avowed intention to substitute dollars for bullets, unilateral intervention by the United States in Latin American affairs had not lessened to the point of promoting new confidence among the Latin American republics.[14] Faced with these circumstances, and their adverse effect upon his work for the Union, Barrett became more and more conciliatory toward the Latin American desire for multilateralism in hemispheric affairs.[15]

Cautiously in the face of disapproval from the State Department, Barrett began to espouse multilateralism in a number of controversial hemispheric issues. Speaking in favor of the Central American Court in 1908, he tied it to the concept of equality in hemispheric cooperation, and called it "the most progressive step toward international arbitration ever taken by a group of governments." [16] A few years later he used the Panama Canal tolls controversy to seek acceptance of his viewpoint:

> While the sentiment is growing that the Canal should be free to vessels flying the United States flag, that arrangement involves grave difficulties with other countries. . . .
> On the ground, moreover, that the United States is making every effort to build up its foreign trade, and inasmuch as such building up depends upon the attitude towards the United States of foreign countries, as well as its own subjective attitude, we must take into consideration the feeling of gratitude that would come to us from foreign countries, especially the twenty republics to the south, if we made the Canal free.[17]

Barrett not only called for the free use of the canal by the Latin American republics. More importantly he associated the canal issue to the Pan Americanization of the Monroe Doctrine:

> Let the United States take advantage of the opening of the Panama

Canal to signalize formally, as it were, the beginning of a new Pan American era in which the Monroe Doctrine, which represents the dictum of one government in a family of nations, shall represent the mutual interest and protection of all.[18]

As early as 1909 Barrett had spoken of the effect of Pan Americanizing the Monroe Doctrine on the Latin American policy of the United States:

As to the Monroe Doctrine, you are going to see in a few years Latin America taking care itself of the Monroe Doctrine. In other words, it will be strong enough of itself so that by combined action it can prevent any possible control of Latin America by monarchical countries. That is the thing we most desire. The more they can look out for themselves, the less talk there will be of United States interference, or the 'Yankee peril' as they call us down there.[19]

The most significant opportunity, however, that Barrett had to expound his interpretation of American policy came as a result of the Mexican Revolution. In 1911 Francisco I. Madero overthrew the Mexican dictatorship of Porfirio Diaz. Unable to consolidate his initial victory and establish a stable government, Madero presided for sixteen long months over the political destruction of the Mexican Republic. Then on February 9, 1913, the counterrevolutionary General Victoriano Huerta came to power following a *coup d'etat.*

Throughout the period of Madero's presidency, the United States and the republics of Latin America had attempted without success to encourage stability in the Mexican Government.[20] In order to begin the quest for a steadying influence in Mexico, John Barrett proposed that the Pan American Union mediate the situation, and thus work to insure an essentially Mexican solution to a Mexican problem. To this end Barrett sent a series of letters on February 13, 1913 to President Taft, President-elect Wilson, and the members of the Senate Foreign Relations Committee explaining his plan.

To avoid the further decay of the Mexican situation, which could eventually lead the United States to intervene with force, Barrett proposed that an international commission of mediation be called under the auspices of the Pan American Union.[22] This commission would be composed of representatives from the United States and the Latin American republics. Barrett suggested that such men as former Secretary of State Elihu Root or the newly designated Secretary of State William Jennings Bryan might represent the United States. From the Latin republics he suggested that the Bolivian Minister to the United States Ignacio Calderon, the Minister to the United States from Uruguay, Dr. Carlos Maria de Pena, or the former provisional president of Mexico, Don Francisco la Barra, could serve the interests of Pan Americanism by laboring on such a peace commission.

Barrett proposed that, once the commission had established a formula for peace, all hostilities in Mexico would cease while the Mexican Government and the revolutionary leaders met to discuss the report of the mediation commission. He reasoned that acceptance of his proposal was the surest means of bringing immediate peace to Mexico, and the first step toward permanent stability and prosperity for the Mexican Government and people "without striking a blow at Mexico's independence and with evidence to all America that the United States [sought] no territorial aggrandizement." [23]

Barrett's immediate objective in calling for mediation was the peace and stability of the Mexican Government. His long range aim, however, was to merge the principles of Pan Americanism with the Monroe Doctrine to create a multilateral hemispheric policy based upon the political equality of all the American republics.[24] In this way the chances of American intervention in Mexico would be considerably lessened, and the cause of Pan Americanism would be served.

Barrett, of course, was not the first American to think along the lines of multilateral Pan Americanism. As discussed above, the seeds of this policy can be found in part in the Latin American policy of former Secretary of State James G. Blaine. Blaine envisioned an organization composed of all the nations of the western hemisphere bound together in the common pursuit of commercial prosperity and political stability. Although his policy was only partially successful, it helped to bring the Monroe Doctrine and Pan Americanism into harmony indirectly by paving the way for enlarging the unilateral scope of the Monroe Doctrine among the American republics.[25] Apparently the intention of his original policy did not call for the political equality of nations, but the concept of Pan Americanism was broad enough to evolve the idea once the hemisphere was confronted by challenges to internal stability.

Although the subject has not been given proper attention in recent years, a number of historians have traced the resulting conflict between unilateral and multilateral interpretations of the Monroe Doctrine in relation to Pan American policy. Some historians have suggested that the announcement of Argentine Foreign Minister Luis Drago's Doctrine in December, 1902, which said that no state had a right to make the financial claims of its citizens against another state the pretext for military intervention, represented Drago's desire for a multilateral policy to supplement the Monroe Doctrine in order to preserve the sovereignty of American republics against unilateral intervention from Europe or elsewhere for financial reasons.[26]

As if in anticipation of the Drago Doctrine, President Theodore Roosevelt declared in his annual message to Congress in December, 1902 that the unilateral interpretation of the Monroe Doctrine was the cardinal principle of American foreign policy.[27] Furthermore, the Roosevelt Corollary to the Monroe Doctrine (1904) announced that the United States had the right to intervene unilaterally in Latin American affairs to preserve order and stability. Thus Roosevelt achieved unilaterally part of what Drago had hoped to gain multilaterally, but it was the United States alone who claimed the right to challenge any interference in Latin America.

Latin Americans were far from pleased with this solution. In order to ease the continued criticism in Latin America against unilateral intervention, the United States sponsored a resolution at the Second Hague Conference in 1907.[28] This resolution made the Drago Doctrine of non-military interference in the internal affairs of Latin American countries a part of international law. By making the principles of the doctrine part of international law it was *in theory* a multilateral guarantee among all nations. But *in fact* the United

States continued to treat Latin America as a private preserve for unilateral intervention under the Monroe Doctrine.[29]

Despite these criticisms of official policies, there were movements in the United States and Latin America to create a genuine multi-lateral Monroe Doctrine. In 1896 Mexican dictator Porfirio Diaz proposed the Pan Americanization of the Monroe Doctrine.[30] Although American interests in Mexico City had worked well with Diaz, he was still fearful of the uses of American power in Latin America. Apparently Diaz's plan was an alternative policy to uni-lateral American intervention and threats of intervention as exempli-fied by American reaction to the Venezuelan boundary dispute with Britain in 1895. The Brazilian diplomat Manuel de Oliveira Lima expressed his desire for a multilateral Pan American policy in *Pan Americanismo* in 1907.[31] But this view of Pan Americanism, which was also put forth by Joaquim Nabuco, the Brazilian Ambassador to the United States (1905–1910), and Domicio da Gama, his succes-sor, was more concerned with establishing a Brazilian-American hegemony in the hemisphere than total political equality among the republics.[32] A more genuine contemporary desire for multilateralism in Latin America can be found in Anibal Maurtua's *La Idea Pan Americana.*[33]

Another aspect of multilateral Pan Americanism concerning mutual guarantees of territorial sovereignty and arbitration procedures among American states has been discussed by a number of historians in connection with the resolutions of Texas Congressman John L. Slay-den in 1910.[34] Similar proposals by the Colombian Minister to London and former President of Colombia, Santiago Perez Triana, in 1912, and Colonel Edward M. House, President Wilson's adviser, in December, 1914 have also been examined.[35]

Some historians have noted John Barrett's speeches and articles in April and July, 1914 in favor of multilateral Pan American pledges of territorial sovereignty without the connotations of domination by the United States.[36] In a recent study, Barrett's Mexican mediation proposal has also been acknowledged in passing.[37]

What is significant about these various proposals according to most of these historians is that they set precedents for and contributed to Woodrow Wilson's Pan American policies as embodied in his Mobile Speech before the Southern Commercial Congress (October 27, 1913) and in the Pan American Pact (December, 1914).[38] Aside from cursory references, these historians have not mentioned the significant, though little recognized, role that John Barrett played in attempting to foster the political equality of the American republics with the United States.

The Washington *Post* was even prepared to attribute to John Barrett at least partial responsibility for Wilson's initial Latin American policies:

> It is interesting to observe a tendency [in the Wilson Administration] to approve a plan first broached by Director General John Barrett of the Pan American Union, which was scoffed at by the previous administration. . . . The Mexican question in its broadest aspect is a Latin American question. It concerns all the nations on this hemisphere. . . . Why should not the United States consult the other nations interested, and act in concert with them? [39]

As early as 1908, Barrett had expressed his belief in the political equality of the American republics:

> The minister of the smallest nation in population has a vote in [the Pan American Union's] governing board equal to that of the Secretary of State of the United States. It is this feature of equal, mutual interest and authority that keeps up the pride of all Latin America in [the Union's] work and advancement.[40]

Barrett had stated that for many years he had been thinking about the relationship between the United States and Latin America.[41] From his previous experience as Minister to Argentina, Panama, and Colombia, and later as Director General of the Pan American Union, Barrett had been aware of the deep resentment of the Latin American republics against the interventionist policies of the United States under the Monroe Doctrine. In order to dispel this resentment, Barrett proposed a revision of the Monroe Doctrine along the lines of a multilateral Pan American doctrine in which each republic, including the United States, would be politically equal in dealing with hemispheric affairs. In other words he wanted a broad Pan

American doctrine modeled after the Pan American Union.

Barrett was not an altruist in propounding the equality of the American republics. He believed that the United States could advance its own enlightened national ends in the hemisphere by abandoning unilateral policy statements and interventions:

> Even if the Latin Americans are not 'overenthusiastic' about the *Monroe Doctrine*, insofar as it suggests our leadership and dominance in the Western Hemisphere, it is unanimous for the *Pan American Doctrine* as a possible substitute for the former. In other words, if you give a Pan American tone to mediation, you will strengthen Mexican confidence in your good intentions and gain the lasting support of the rest of Latin America.[42]

The scramble for markets in Latin America among the European industrial nations and the success of commercial expansion were closely interwoven with political domination over the territory that was being exploited. A debtor nation's political existence depended upon keeping favor with the creditor nation. In the past the United States had to watch carefully European influence in Latin America and be ready to intervene unilaterally to restore stability if national independence was threatened as a result of commercial and financial dependence.

By adopting a multilateral Pan American policy in place of a unilateral Monroe Doctrine, Barrett believed that the United States would be able to counteract European influence and be assured of the political and economic stability and progress of the hemisphere.[43] The creation of a genuine community of Pan American interests based upon equality could be used to marshall the moral and material resources of the hemisphere to maintain the sovereignty of its members from external and internal threats without alienating the Latin American republics in the way that unilateral intervention by the United States had done in the past. This was ultimately the underlying principle behind the Pan American mediation plan which he submitted to President Taft and President-elect Wilson in February, 1913—long before Wilson's Mobile Speech (October 27, 1913) or the Pan American Pact (December, 1914).[44]

Unfortunately for Barrett, he decided to make his plan available to the press in order to gain public support for his proposal before receiving a reply from the Administration or the State Department. This set off a storm of controversy. The *Mexican Herald,* the New Orleans *Item,* Panama *Star and Herald,* and *La Prensa* (Buenos Aires) carried stories of protest from the Society of the American Colony in Mexico City.[45] The Society had called for the use of forceful, "energetic action" by the United States in Mexico.[46] Barrett's proposal for new discussions threatened to hinder its efforts. American Ambassador Henry Lane Wilson voiced his anger over what he termed Barrett's interference in strictly State Department business.[47] Wilson had been working hard for the recognition of the Huerta regime by the United States. Barrett's mediation offer jeopardized his position.

In response tn this criticism, Barrett claimed in a press interview that "intervention advocates . . . gratuitously misunderstood his plan." [48] He then revealed that, on February 15, he received an anonymous letter warning him against two alleged powers in the government who opposed his plan. One power wanted intervention and American military occupation in Mexico; the other power was the head of a government department who personally disliked Barrett. When questioned further about the letter, Barrett said that he did not take it seriously and destroyed it. The press, however, immediately interpreted the two powers in opposition to Barrett to be Secretary of State Philander C. Knox, and Assistant Secretary of State Francis M. Huntington-Wilson.[49] For some time Barrett had differed with Knox on the Secretary's idea of "preventive intervention" in Latin America, and his high-handed attitude in dealing with the Latin republics. The fact that much of the formulation and execution of Knox's policies had been attributed to Huntington-Wilson caused Barrett to be quite wary of him as well.[50]

Despite this official antagonism, editorials in support of Pan American Union mediation appeared in a number of newspapers and magazines. The Washington *Times* had been openly critical of American diplomacy in Latin America during the Taft Administration.[51]

It considered Barrett's peace plan the most practical alternative. The *Christian Science Monitor* remarked: "What has come up for decision is the question of whether the American shall henceforth be regarded as the conquering Anglo-Saxon, or be definitely established as first among his peers . . . of the western world." [52]

The Detroit *News* attacked the concept of "dollar diplomacy," which it said formed an alliance between Wall Street and corrupt regimes in Latin America.[53] Pan American mediation, as opposed to past policies, offered hope for the future. The New York *World* had proposed mediation itself, but admitted that Barrett's plan was more acceptable because it included representatives from Latin America.[54] *The Independent* said that Pan American mediation deserved a more careful consideration than it had been given. *The Outlook* gave its support to Barrett's proposal as well.[55]

Barrett also received letters from various individuals and organizations congratulating him on his proposal. Hamilton Holt, editor of *The Independent,* wrote that he would personally endorse Pan American mediation. Elihu Root noted that while Barrett had good intentions the situation had reached such a critical stage that any affirmative suggestion would have difficulty gaining acceptance. Other letters of support were received from the Anti-Imperialist League; Albert Shaw, editor of the *Review of Reviews;* J. B. Tait, president of the Washington and Southern Bank; Walter Hines Page; L. L. Seamen, head of the China Society of America; W. P. Massie, president of the Mexican branch of the Equitable Life Assurance Society of the United States; and Frank A. Vanderlip and W. Morgan Shuster of the National City Bank of New York.[56]

A number of endorsements, some rather reserved, were obtained from Latin American diplomats and officials including those from Salvador Castrillo of Nicaragua, Ignatio Calderon, Bolivian Minister to the United States, Francisco H. Pezet of Peru, Manuel de Oliveira Lima, Brazilian Minister to Great Britain, and Angel C. Rivas, former Assistant Secretary of State of Venezuela.[57] Barrett also had the support of practically all the members of the Governing Board of the Pan American Union.[58]

Perhaps the most interesting letter came from Heriberto Barron, the former editor of the Mexico City daily *El Liberal*, and now a commercial agent in the United States for the Mexican Government.[59] Some months before Barrett's proposal was made public, Barron had confidentially submitted his own plan to President Madero and President Taft. In it he called for a convention to meet at San Antonio, Texas composed of representatives from all political factions in Mexico, and leading American politicians and businessmen for the purpose of mediating an end to the war. At that time both Madero and Taft refused to comment on Barron's scheme.

Apparently unknown to both Barrett and Barron was the fact that the United States and Mexico tried to bring about a meeting in San Antonio between Mexican and American representatives at the same time that Barrett's Pan American Union mediation plan was made public. This attempt by the Taft Administration failed to win the support of the Mexican insurrectionists and the entire conference fell through.[60] This may explain, in part, why Taft was not receptive to Barrett's peace plan.

But even beyond this was the fear that Barrett's proposal would be regarded in Latin America as a step toward formulating a new Pan American policy based on multilateralism as a substitute for the Monroe Doctrine. Taft confided in a press interview that this was the strongest reason for rejection.[61] Privately the President wrote to Barrett that he regretted the situation into which he had been placed, and assured him that their friendship would continue.[62]

American policy toward Mexico under the Taft Administration, and under the Wilson Administration as well, was geared toward mediation; but it was mediation under the unilateral leadership of the United States, not multilateral mediation under the aegis of the Pan American Union. Yet even though Barrett had been overruled by the administrations of Taft and Wilson, he actively supported Woodrow Wilson's attempts at unilateral mediation.[63] This was preferable, after all, to no attempt to stabilize the situation in Mexico.

With the failure of unilateral mediation and Wilson's policy of "watchful waiting," the willingness to use forceful intervention by the Wilson Administration was intensified. By July, 1913 Secretary of State William Jennings Bryan noted that the deep interest of the United States in Latin American conditions necessitated the real possibility of this alternative.[64] Bryan, however, was distressed that this might come to pass. Although John Barrett continued to plead with President Wilson to adopt a broader multilateral Pan American policy to safeguard the prestige and commerce of the United States in Latin America, he gave the full support of the Pan American Union to Wilson's narrower mediation attempts.[65]

Actually Wilson's initial policy decision in favor of an exclusively North American solution to the Mexican problem came in response to a plan suggested in May, 1913 by several American corporations with large holdings in Mexico—the Southern Pacific Railroad, Phelps, Dodge & Company, Greene Cananea Copper Company, and Edward L. Doheny's Mexican Petroleum Company.[66] They advised that the State Department should agree to recognize Huerta if Huerta held a presidential election by October 23, 1913. The constitutionalists, led by Venustiano Carranza, were to suspend hostilities against Huerta, participate in the election, and agree to support whomever was elected president.

Wilson was impressed by this proposal, and in June, 1913, he sent a special agent to Mexico, William Bayard Hale, to gain information as to whether or not the plan should be implemented. From what he learned, Wilson set two conditions for a peaceful settlement to the Mexican Revolution: first, Huerta had to agree to hold constitutional elections, and second, Huerta had to agree not to be a candidate himself for president. If these conditions were met, the United States would attempt to mediate between the warring factions.[67]

To present his conditions to Huerta, Wilson sent John Lind, the former governor of Minnesota, as his personal representative. Lind told Huerta that if he would not run for office, and fair elections were held based upon constitutional procedures, the United States would be willing to mediate an end to the war. But Huerta adamantly refused any form of American intervention. Lind then offered to arrange a loan between the United States and the new Mexican government if Huerta would agree to his offer. Huerta was outraged by this, and demanded that Lind leave the country.[68]

With the failure of Lind's mission, the President announced a policy of "watchful waiting" on August 17, 1913. For a while it looked as if the Mexicans might be able to solve their own problems, but in October Huerta instituted a complete military dictatorship.[69] With this move, Wilson revealed publicly in his Mobile Speech that he now deemed the possibility of intervention greater than ever when he indirectly suggested that the United States was about to launch a campaign against Huerta.[70] Although the address also contained a brief statement of the United States' belief in Pan Americanism, Arthur S. Link, the foremost scholar of Wilsonian diplomacy, has written:

> There is no evidence that Wilson, Bryan, or Lansing was prepared to do more than pay lip service to the Pan American ideal. . . . Nor were they ready to denounce the so-called right of intervention.[71]

Some years after the events of 1913 Robert Lansing made a similar observation:

> The President is a phrase-maker par excellence. He admires trite sayings and revels in formulating them. But when it comes to their practical application he is so vague that their worth may well be doubted. He apparently never thought out in advance where they would lead or how they would be interpreted by others. . . . The gift of clever phrasing may be a curse unless the phrases are put to the test of sound, practical application before being uttered.[72]

Indeed, despite the rhetoric at Mobile, from November, 1913 to April, 1914, Wilson worked to isolate Huerta diplomatically, and encourage Carranza's Constitutionalists to seize power. Under American pressure, Britain withdrew its recognition of the Huerta Government.[73] In February, the United States lifted its arms embargo and began making weapons available to the Constitutionalists. The situation between Mexico and the United States deteriorated to such a degree that the United States used an incident involving the arrest of American sailors by Mexican officials at Tampico as an excuse to fire upon and occupy Vera Cruz on April 21, 1914.[74]

Almost immediately the diplomatic representatives of Argentina, Brazil, and Chile offered to mediate before full scale war developed.[75] On April 29, Huerta and Carranza accepted mediation, and Niagara Falls, Ontario was designated for the conference. [6]

Wilson agreed to mediation, but never really intended to abide by it. On the contrary, Wilson planned to use mediation as a "means of eliminating Huerta and establishing a provisional government that would turn Mexico over to the Constitutionalists." [77]

On July 15, 1914 Huerta resigned, and Carranza assumed power on August 20. Wilson, however, was still not satisfied because Carranza refused to permit him to use A.B.C. mediation as a means of imposing a political program on Mexico dictated by the United States.[78] Wilson thought he could advance his ends by supporting Pancho Villa as an alternative to Carranza, but this strategy failed. When Carranza finally emerged as the strongest force in 1915, Argentina, Bolivia, Brazil, Chile, Guatemala, Uruguay, and the United States agreed to the *de facto* recognition of the Carranza regime on October 19. Fighting among Mexican factions continued, however, until 1917 when Carranza consolidated his power and was recognized as the legally elected president.

In accepting the mediation of the Latin American republics, Wilson once again had assumed the mantle of Pan Americanism in place of direct intervention for the unilateral ends of the United States. Less than three months after the *de facto* recognition of the Carranza Government, Wilson stated the independence of the United States from multilateral hemispheric policies:

> The Monroe Doctrine was proclaimed by the United States on her own authority. It has always been maintained, and always will be maintained, upon her own responsibility.[79]

In June, 1914, Robert Lansing, then Counselor for the State Department, commented upon the rationale of the United States for the Monroe Doctrine and its relation to Pan American policy:

The opposition of European control over American territory is not primarily to preserve the independence of any American state—that may be the result, but not the purpose of the [Monroe] Doctrine. The essential idea is to prevent a condition which would menace the national interests of the United States. [The Monroe Doctrine was founded upon] the superior power of the United States to compel submission to its will whenever a condition arises involving European control over American territory. . . . To assert for it a nobler purpose is to proclaim a new doctrine.[80]

Lansing did not advise that the United States should end its Pan American policy. He simply pointed out that to merge it with the Monroe Doctrine, thus producing a hemisphere of equal partners, would allow other nations to pass upon the judgments of the United States.[81] The Monroe Doctrine had to remain apart from Pan Americanism in order to maintain American freedom of action and a sense of national priorities.[82]

This expression of the singlemindedness of American policy in the western hemisphere may appear as a contradiction in the light of later Pan American solutions to the Mexican situation. Actually the shift in American tactics in favor of a pseudo-Pan Americanism was brought about in part by a consideration of American policy *vis-a-vis* Germany, and the World War in Europe and its effect in the western hemisphere.

In a policy memorandum dated October 10, 1915, Robert Lansing noted that Germany did not want any one faction dominant in Mexico.[83] American policy, therefore, had to be geared to the recognition of one dominant political faction in Mexico to bring about stability, and remove Germany's opportunity to exploit the situation. In the final analysis American policy came down to this:

Our possible relations with Germany must be our first consideration, and all our intercourse with Mexico must be regulated accordingly. It is the only rational and safe policy under present conditions, but we might as well understand that the American people will not approve of it, though the future may and, I have no doubt, will justify the wisdom of the course adopted.[84]

John Barrett agreed with the ends of the State Department as they were presented by Robert Lansing. He felt, however, that it was necessary to employ different means by drawing the Latin American republics closer to the United States with a genuine Pan American doctrine. The unilateralism of the Monroe Doctrine succeeded in causing ill-will and suspicion. Through Pan Americanism the United States could maintain hemispheric hegemony without the unilateral periodic use of force.[85] This was Barrett's long range strategy in advocating multilateral Pan American mediation of the Mexican revolution.

In addition Barrett believed that if the United States could develop an expanded trade program with the nations of Latin America, and mutual economic bonds, a harmony of economic and political interests would result. Gradually European interests would be phased out of Latin American affairs, and the United States would command the commercial and political leadership of the western hemisphere without contest. The industrial and scientific progress of the United States had placed it in a naturally favored position to exploit Latin American resources. But the benefits of this relationship would not fall to the United States without a conscious, organized effort to achieve them.[86]

With the advent of the First World War in Europe, Barrett saw a great opportunity for the United States. As a result of the war and the great demands that it made on the participants, the markets in Latin America for European manufactures had fallen to American industries. As far as Barrett was concerned, there was no reason why the United States could not hold on to these markets after the war. But the real key to success was the development of a viable Pan American policy—a multilateral doctrine of equality for the Americas.[87]

The war in Europe was to Barrett "God's War" for it created the necessary conditions to insure that the balance of power between Europe and Asia would fall to the United States upon its conclusion.[88] While the European powers were fighting, the United States could develop its industrial and commercial strength in Latin America to an unchallengeable position. This development would have ramifications for the United States throughout the world. The United States, however, had to prepare for this situation by initiating adequate policies. The place to begin was in Latin America.

Barrett worked long and hard to cultivate and enlarge American interest in Latin America. In addition to his duties as a diplomat, publicist, and Director General of the Pan American Union, he was also a founder of the Pan American Society of the United States. This was a social, cultural, and commercial organization modelled after the American Asiatic Society, and designed to further the bonds of Pan Americanism. Formed in 1911, its membership was composed of noted diplomats, bankers, exporters, industrialists, publishers, and educators.[89] Some of its more prominent members were Henry White, Ambassador to France, as president of the Society, Lloyd C. Griscom, Ambassador to Japan and Brazil, as vice-president; and Cabot Ward, as secretary. Its governing board was composed of such men as Nicholas Murray Butler, president of Columbia University, James A. Farrell of United States Steel Corporation, John Bassett Moore, noted jurist and State Department adviser, and Lewis Nixon, president of the United States Shipbuilding Company and the New York Board of Trade.[90] Unfortunately the Society declined after American intervention in the Mexican Revolution. By 1916 Barrett withdrew as an active force in the Society.[91]

Barrett, however, remained active as a promoter of Pan Americanism over and above his official duties with the Pan American Union. In a private capacity he served as president of the advisory council of the Pan American College of Commerce in Panama.[92] The College was established by the Southern Commercial Congress. Its student body was drawn from chambers of commerce, boards of trade, corporations, and educational institutions desiring to establish foreign trade marketing and financial investment as parts of their organizational training programs.

One of Barrett's most significant accomplishments while Director General of the Union was his work in organizing the Second Pan American Scientific Congress held in Washington in 1915 and 1916.[93] Barrett had envisioned cultural, political, and economic progress through the scientific management and mobilization of the hemisphere's material resources and production capacity.[94] In working to achieve these ends, the Congress accomplished a great deal. It dealt with the standardization of weights and measures. railway construction, communications, electronics, navigation, the improvement of agricultural and conservation methods, aeronautics, medicine and sanitation, engineering, education, and international law.[95] With the compilation of such a vast body of knowledge, Barrett looked forward to a hemisphere, and eventually a world, composed of efficient and progressive societies.

A significant extension of the Pan American Scientific Congress came about with the entrance of the United States into the First World War in 1917. Although Barrett did not think any benefits would be obtained by the United States as a result of its participation in the war, he did hope to contribute to an Allied victory by putting forth a plan to make use of the knowledge acquired from the Scientific Congress and the Pan American Union. To this end he proposed the creation of a Special Pan American Advisory Council to marshall the resources of Latin America behind the American and Allied war efforts.[96]

According to his plan, the United States would create an advisory council of American authorities on political, financial, commercial, economic, and military conditions in Latin America.[97] The council was not to be independent, but subordinate to the State Department. All knowledge compiled by these experts would then be given to the Council of National Defense, the War and Naval Departments, the Shipping and War Trade Boards, and the Food and Fuel Administrations. To insure that his proposal received wide attention, Barrett sent letters explaining his plan to the President, State Department, and all the war administrations. Responses poured in immediately from Administration progressives.

Herbert Hoover, chairman of the Food Administration, wrote "I cordially agree that your plan is a good one, and have no doubt that it will be successful if you are to organize it yourself." [98] Harry Garfield, chairman of the Fuel Administration and the son of Pres-

ident James A. Garfield, was enthusiastic about the plan, and remarked that it was the sort of thing that his father's administration
would have supported.[99]

Letters endorsing the creation of the Pan American Advisory
Council came from Frank Scott, chairman of the War Industries
Board, George Creel, chairman of the Committee on Public Informa-
tion, Bernard Baruch, commissioner of raw materials for the War
Industries Board, W. S. Clifford, chairman of the Council of National
Defense, David F. Houston, Secretary of Agriculture, and Edward
N. Hurley, chairman of the Shipping Board.[100]

Secretary of State Lansing and President Wilson did not accept
the proposal, however, because they felt that the creation of such
a council would be considered a form of coercion by the United
States against the neutral Latin American republics.[101] Unfortunately
the Administration and the State Department seemed to be more
influenced by the distorted report of Barrett's proposal written by
Albert W. Fox in the Washington *Post.*[102] Fox's article had made
it appear as if Barrett wanted to club the Latin American republics
into supporting the United States in the war. This report also incensed
the Latin American representatives to the United States, who were
worried about Barrett's executive prerogative in proposing his plan
without consultation with the Union's Governing Board.[103]

Another criticism against Barrett according to the Administration
was that the Director General of the Pan American Union was in
theory a neutral international official.[104] Barrett's plan disclosed the
Union to be a partisan of the American cause. The Administration's
position on this criticism, however, was inconsistant in view of the
fact that Secretary of the Treasury William McAdoo and Charles
Horner, director of the Speakers' Bureau of the War Loan Organization, enlisted Barrett in the Administration's Liberty Loan drive
without the issue of Barrett's neutral position being raised.[105]

In addition Barrett continued to speak out in favor of the expansion
of American markets in Latin America as he had always done.
Certainly this could have been easily construed as partisan activity,
but the Wilson Administration was never critical of this practice.

In fact Wilson reversed his earlier stand against dollar diplomacy as attested by the passage of the Webb-Pomerene Act (1918), the Second Pan American Commercial Conference (1919), and the reentry of the United States into the China consortium (1917).[106]

In a speech entitled "Latin American Trade—A Comparative View," Barrett gave a clue to the renewed encouragement of commercial expansion by the Wilson Administration.[107] He noted that many American manufacturers would rather stay at home in the domestic market than gamble in foreign markets. It was only with the efficient production of the modern industrial economy that trade expansion began on a large scale. As a result of the First World War, American production had become even more efficient. In connection with this process Barrett offered the economic axiom that "Real efficiency soon bursts domestic bonds." The United States had little choice, according to Barrett's argument, except to seek greater international commerce in response to industrial and technological advancements. In reply to this speech, Edward N. Hurley congratulated Barrett on being an advocate of efficiency and a member of the progressive establishment.[108]

To be sure, John Barrett was a progressive. One of his last memoranda as Director General of the Pan American Union called for the enactment of conservation laws throughout the nations of Latin America to protect their natural wealth from the selfish exploitation of foreign capital including that of the United States.[109]

Another proposal in the progressive tradition was Barrett's plan to expand the Pan American Union into a hemispheric "league of nations." In a memorandum to President Wilson entitled "The Pan American Union—A Working League of Nations." Barrett outlined his plan:

> Although the Pan American Council lacks the specific delegated authority of the constituent governments to negotiate and preserve peace among them, and its practical power is limited to moral suasion . . . an international resolution or treaty, drafted and signed at the next or Fifth International Conference of the American Republics and then approved by the Congresses of all the American governments, would convert this council . . . into a Pan American League with actual power to prevent war

and preserve peace, with . . . authority to initiate mediation or arbitration between would-be belligerents.[110]

In a second note to the President, Barrett noted that the trend of developments in the hemisphere pointed to what he was now suggesting:

> Looking back over the various Pan American Conferences which have been held since the first one at Washington in 1889–1890 . . . and then bearing in mind the informal discussions that have taken place from year to year among the members of the Governing Board . . . it can be authoritatively said that there is a strong underlying opinion that the powers of the Governing Board . . . or some other body representing the American republics should have the authority of the American governments to initiate mediation, and to enforce, to a certain degree, respect for their decisions.[111]

What Barrett really wanted to accomplish with his Pan American League was the standardization of authorized procedures to insure maximum political stability in the hemisphere.

President Wilson replied to Barrett's suggestions that he did not think it would be wise to divide the world into two peace-keeping organizations.[112] One League of Nations was enough to serve the entire world. Wilson felt that the League and the Union would interfere with each other's tasks if the role of the Union was broadened. Thus the President put aside Barrett's scheme for a regional political organization in favor of one that was centralized on a world-wide basis.

Consumed by his passion for the League, Wilson failed to see that a regional association could be useful to his overall purpose of establishing machinery for international peace. The goals of the League and Barrett's proposed political goals for the Union were not dissimilar. In fact they complemented each other. Even if the Pan American Union had been given a subordinate role in relation to the League of Nations instead of exclusive sovereignty in the western hemisphere, the Union could have aided the League in the administration of hemispheric affairs.

In 1948 American policy makers accepted the role of the Pan

American Union as a regional organization in relation to another world body, the United Nations. The charter of the Organization of American States drawn up in Bogota contained four articles which, in effect, realized the reforms suggested by Barrett:

> *Article 20.* All international disputes that may arise between American states shall be submitted to the peaceful procedures set forth in this charter before being referred to the Security Council of the United Nations.

> *Article 21.* The following are peaceful procedures: direct negotiation, good offices, mediation, investigation and conciliation, judicial settlement, arbitration, and those which the parties to the dispute may especially agree upon at any time.

> *Article 22.* In the event that a dispute arises between two or more American states which, in the opinion of one of them, cannot be settled through the usual diplomatic channels, the parties shall agree on some other peaceful procedure that will enable them to reach a solution.

> *Article 23.* A Special Treaty will establish adequate procedures for the pacific settlement of disputes . . . so that no dispute between American states shall fail of definitive settlement within a reasonable period.[113]

As long as the United States maintained a separate policy toward Latin America, the Pan American Union served special American needs. Given the trend of greater involvement by the United States in Latin America, it was practically inevitable that the Union would become more political in nature as American political and commercial interests grew.

Unfortunately for Barrett, he virtually assured the end of his tenure as Director General of the Pan American Union by the submission of his proposal to the press in April, 1919.[114] This characteristic attempt to gain public support predictably failed to succeed. Unable to achieve his major goal, Barrett submitted his resignation in he fall of 1919, and in September, 1920 he officially stepped down as Director General of the Pan American Union.

In a letter to his mother, Barrett claimed that he was retiring for financial reasons.[115] For years he had worked without putting away a penny in anticipation of his old age. Now he was resigning to become a private consultant on Pan American commerce in order to command the high fees he was capable of earning in that capacity.

In reality, however, Barrett had outlived his usefulness to the Wilson Administration. All through the years of Wilson's Presidency, he and Barrett had clashed over the question of Barrett's authority and the scope of the Pan American Union in political affairs. Such issues as the Mexican Revolution, Pan Americanization of the Monroe Doctrine, and the Pan American Advisory Council proposal during World War I had driven Barrett and the Administration and State Department wide apart. Barrett's call for a Pan American League of Nations was the final blow to his security as Director General.

In addition, Barrett's egoism and grandiloquent sytle had alienated not only the President but other high officials as well including Secretary of the Treasury William McAdoo.[116] Personal friction certainly gave impetus to the reasons for Barrett's dismissal. With Barrett's resignation in hand, the Administration moved quickly to appoint a new Director General. Rumors were already spreading that Barrett planned to launch a campaign to name his own successor. Although Secretary of State Bainbridge Colby did not believe such rumors to be true, he did advise Wilson to make an early selection.[117] The choice was Leo S. Rowe, head of the Latin American Division of the State Department, and a former professor of Latin American studies at the University of Pennsylvania.

Another important reason for the demand for Barrett's resignation at this time came from within the Pan American Union itself. Barrett's inability to work with the State Department as a result of his objectionable political proposals made him a liability to the member states of the Pan American Union.[118] With the State Department and the Union increasingly at odds, the Latin American republics could expect little in the way of cooperation and favorable treatment from the State Department.

To this reason must be added the fact that the Governing Board of the Pan American Union had become dissatisfied with Barrett as a result of his unilateral proposal to establish an Advisory Council to aid the Allied war effort in 1917.[119] This dissatisfaction continued to grow in the next two years. The main point at issue was that of defining the exact powers of the Director General, and those of the Governing Board. The fact that Barrett had begun planning the Second Pan American Commercial Congress with the State and Treasury Departments in March, 1919 without consulting the Governing Board set off a new wave of opposition within the Union.[120] Following from this was the general question of whether the Director General had the right to speak for the Union without direct authorization from the Governing Board.[121] The total effect of all these divisive forces convinced Barrett that the existence of the Pan American Union itself depended upon his resignation.[122] Alternatives no longer existed for him. He had only one choice.

During Barrett's last few months as Director General, he received fitting tribute from friends and well-wishers. George M. Cornwall, editor of the Portland trade journal *Timberman* wrote, "the United States will never know how much it owes to the Director General's inspirations in bringing the peoples of Latin America into closer and more harmonious relations with this country."[123] Charles Schnabel, a Portland lawyer, noted that more than anyone else Barrett had "opened up trade relations between Portland and some of the South American Republics." [124] H. Daniels of International Harvester wrote:

> It is my opinion that comparatively few citizens of this country realize the importance or the extent of the work which has been accomplished in improving the relations between the United States and Latin American countries. You have made commercial business possible in many places where without your efforts nothing could have been done. . . . To you personally, more than to any other individual or group of individuals, is due the credit of this wonderful development of the relations between the Pan American countries.[125]

Other letters of praise came from Arthur Bullard, chief of the Russian Affairs Division of the State Department, A. F. DuPont of DuPont Foods, and the World Trade Club.[126] One noteworthy farewell was received from Homer Brett, the American Consul in Santiago, Chile, who not only spoke highly of Barrett's work as a commercial publicist and diplomat, but excused him of any errors of judgment as well:

> We have the trade of Latin American in measure full and running over, not only to a value greater than anyone ever expected, but even greater than you ever predicted. . . . I have decided that your course was dictated by the highest wisdom and that no criticism is due. . . . Surely upon such work as this no man with reason and a conscience can give you any other verdict than 'well done.' [127]

In September, 1920 John Barrett left the Pan American Union and an historic era behind him. Constitutionally the organization had not changed very much during the long years of his leadership. The Union had been brought up to its full potential, however, as an organ of commercial and industrial expansion and progress among the nations of the western hemisphere.

Barrett had served the interests of Pan Americanism well. But when he tried to take the next step beyond economic growth—the step of Pan American political equality—too quickly, he moved beyond his immediate era and out of the political picture. In time, however, American leadership would come to see the wisdom of Barrett's proposals for mutual Pan Americanism as the most acceptable means of maintaining the hegemony of the United States in the western hemisphere.

5. The Last Years of an Elder Statesman, 1920–1938

THE last eighteen years of John Barrett's life were filled with disapointments that were very difficult to bear even for a natural-born optimist. Despite Barrett's desire to return to public life in the capacity of a front-line diplomat or elected official, he found that doors were closed to his aspirations. Shortly after leaving the Pan American Union, he received a special appointment as a newspaper correspondent for *El Universal* of Mexico City to cover the Washington Disarmament Conference in 1921.[1]

In this capacity he was quite strong in his criticism of the fact that no Latin American republics were represented at the Conference.[2] Naturally State Department officials were not pleased with Barrett's reports, and they grew more incensed when he suggested in his articles that the resignation of Henry P. Fletcher as Ambassador to Mexico in 1921 meant that the United States would recognize the Obregon Government.[3] This episode virtually slammed the door shut on any future diplomatic appointments.

Barrett's inability to get another diplomatic post was not the only defeat he suffered. Even before he became a special correspondent for *El Universal* he had set himself up in Washington as a private consultant on Pan American affairs. There were few calls for Barrett's services, however, and within a year after opening his office he was forced to give up the venture.[4] Taking to the lecture circuit once again, as the one and only member of the "Pan American Committee," Barrett prepared a number of speeches and memoranda on Pan American policies. Drawing upon his experiences, he proceeded to offer his insights, in the hope of gaining an appointment, to the Republican President-elect Warren Harding just as he had submitted his Mexican peace plan to President-elect Wilson in 1913.[5]

Unlike Wilson, Harding was receptive and invited Barrett to confer with the newly designated Secretary of State, Charles Evans Hughes. In these discussions Barrett was particularly concerned about the prompt recognition of the Mexican Government, the withdrawal of American receivership in Haiti and the Dominican Republic, senatorial approval of the treaty to reimburse Colombia for the loss of Panama, and multilateral talks to end the half-century Tacna-Arica dispute between Chile and Peru.[6] It is not known what value Hughes placed on these talks, but whatever personal gain might have come to Barrett through these discussions was lost after his critical reports for *El Universal*. It is quite probable that these criticisms were more caustic as a result of the Harding Administration's failure to make Barrett an offer of appointment.

After his term of employment with *El Universal* ended in 1922, Barrett espoused a number of minor Pan American causes in order to keep his name before the public. One of particular importance to him personally was the centennial celebration of the Monroe Doctrine in 1923:

> Our . . . recommendation has been that . . . commemorations of the event should avoid as much as possible any political or partisan interpretation of the Monroe Doctrine and its political influence on Latin American and Pan American affairs. Instead we have urged that they be devoted as far as possible to a review and appraisement of the extraordinary progress of the Pan American countries in cultural, intellectual and social, as well as material, economic and commercial achievement, and to the influence of . . . Pan American solidarity . . . upon the . . . western hemisphere and [the] world.[7]

But once again the State Department was unresponsive to his

suggestion. In 1924 Barrett also tried to interest the Department in making Columbus Day a Pan American holiday. Although the Department itself did not endorse the proposal, Francis White, chief of the Latin American Division, thought it was an excellent idea:

> I think the suggestion to make Columbus Day . . . a Pan American Day is a good one. October 12 is celebrated throughout Latin America as "El Dia de la Raza"—the day of the race—as an attempt to show the fraternal bonds of consanguinity between Spain and its Latin American countries. As we also have some claim to Columbus I think it would be well to try to make it a Pan American rather than a Hispano-American event.[8]

This sort of publicizing was calculated to keep Barrett's name in the news until a major opportunity arose for real recognition. In May, 1926 Barrett thought he had that opportunity for it was then that he announced himself a Republican candidate for the Senate from Vermont.[9] Since President Coolidge was a fellow native Vermonter, and well acquainted with his work, Barrett was hoping that he could persuade the President and the state Republican machinery to give their endorsements, but instead former Governor W. W. Strickney received the President's support, and Barrett quickly withdrew from the race.

Having made the initial overture to Coolidge, Barrett persisted in seeking a presidential favor. This time he requested an appointment as ambassador either to Cuba, Brazil, or Chile.[10] But once again he was rebuffed.[11]

With the advent of the Hoover Administration in 1929, Barrett again sought official recognition. He proposed a plan to follow up Hoover's Good Will Tour of Latin America with a scholarship program to encourage research into the future development of Pan Americanism. To this suggestion Hoover was quite cool, and told Barrett plainly that he had his own policies and did not appreciate any interference.[12] In retaliation Barrett openly attacked the protectionist Smoot-Hawley Tariff of 1930 as a handicap to Pan American trade in a letter to the editor of the New York *Times*.[13]

The New York *Times* was practically the only forum that Barrett had left. A heart condition kept him from continuing his strenuous lecture tours, and in 1930 he retired to Coral Gables, Florida. Over the remaining eight years of his life he wrote on such topics as Soviet commercial competition in Latin America, the Cuban Revolution, multilateral mediation of the Chaco War (1932), and reciprocity.

On the issue of expanding Soviet economic competition in Latin America, Barrett called for closer economic union among the nations of the western hemisphere:

> The United States and its sister American nations will achieve little by assailing communism, alleged Soviet propaganda and emphasizing their danger. The Americans will, on the other hand, at once take a mighty step forward to meet Russian competition for domination of new and Old World affairs by discussing, planning and developing practical plans and powerful agencies for cooperation.[14]

The logical extension of Barrett's remarks was a revision of the tariff in the United States away from protectionism in order to promote North American trade with Latin America. To Barrett's mind reciprocity was the answer.

The outbreak of the Cuban Revolution in 1931 offered Barrett another opportunity to speak out. As expected, Barrett opposed the possibility of American intervention:

> The chief threat in the acute Cuban crisis is to the United States and not to Cuba! The anomalous situation develops from the stark possibility of . . . intervention by United States armed forces. Such action by the United States, no matter how seemingly justified . . . by lawlessness endangering lives and property, might prove the greatest disaster in the history of Pan Americanism!
>
> Armed United States intervention would never be understood . . . by the other nineteen sister republics of the Pan American family. It would do immeasurable harm to Pan Americanism. . . . It might nullify completely . . . the recent pronouncement of President Hoover through Secretary Stimson against armed interventions. It might, in short, be a staggering . . . blow to . . . Western Hemisphere solidarity . . . in facing the . . . economic and political competition and power of Europe and Soviet Russia.[15]

Given the threat of unilateral action by the United States in Cuba,

Barrett was particularly pleased with Argentine Foreign Minister Saavedra Lamas' call for Latin American mediation of the Chaco War in 1932 between Bolivia and Paraguay.[16] According to Barrett, Argentina had offered a model of Pan Americanism for the United States to follow in all future relations with Latin America.

Another of Barrett's recurrent criticisms was aimed at the protective tariff policies of the United States. Unfavorable trade policies were as detrimental to Pan Americanism as armed intervention. For the persistent troubles of economic stagnation in the hemisphere Barrett prescribed reciprocity in measured doses.[17] It would not be long before this remedy was put into effect.

Faced with the propsect of Franklin Roosevelt's presidency after the election of 1932, Barrett was pleased to offer his suggestions on Pan American policies to his old acquaintance. In a letter of April 8, 1933 Barrett suggested "a considerable measure of real reciprocity" as the best way to improve trade relations.[18] In September Barrett again wrote the President in support of non-intervention in the Cuban Revolution, and the abrogation of the Platt Amendment.[19] In October he endorsed diplomatic recognition of the Soviet Union to enhance trade prospects and ease international tensions.[20] Whether or not Roosevelt paid heed to Barrett's advice is not known with certainty, but his Good Neighbor Policy toward Latin America was clearly in tune with Barrett's long-standing program. Barrett did receive letters of acknowledgment from Assistant Secretary of State Sumner Welles, and Secretary of State Cordell Hull, the Administration's champion for reciprocity.[21] Hull was especially cordial in writing:

> I know of no one better informed on this general Latin American situation, or more capable of commenting wisely and soundly than yourself. I am correspondingly glad, therefore, to have the benefit of any message or any suggestions that you may be good enough to offer from time to time.[22]

But despite Barrett's deep involvement with Latin America and his desire for official recognition during the next two years, he withdrew from Latin American affairs. In November, 1934 at the age of sixty-eight he married (for the first time) Mary Elizabeth Cady, the widow of an old friend from Burlington, Vermont.[23] The marriage was essentially that of a business arrangement whereby Barrett took over management of family properties for the former Mrs. Cady. After the wedding the couple left for an extended tour of Europe, where they visited the Soviet Union, Czechoslovakia, France, Italy, Switzerland, and Germany.

With their return to the United States in 1936, Barrett began lecturing on Pan American affairs once again. In a speech prepared for the Pan American League in Miami, Barrett exhibited a great deal of satisfaction in the work of the Roosevelt Administration in Latin America at the time of the Buenos Aires Conference:

> President Roosevelt and Secretary Hull are initiating a program no less momentous than the Monroe Doctrine, . . . and yet, if this Buenos Aires Conference culminates in any one great achievement, it will be possibly the substitution of what might be called a "Pan American Doctrine" to take the place of the Monroe Doctrine. . . . it may mean that all the unpopular features of the Monroe Doctrine as it suggested paternalism on the part of the United States towards other American nations, will be evolved into a united western hemisphere policy, . . . having as its central thought that all of the American republics and not merely the United States, will stand together to protect the independence of any one American republic from European invasion or attack.
>
> But the chief purpose of this unprecedented inter-American meeting will be the maintenance of permanent peace on the Western Hemisphere through the combined and unanimous action of all the American republics.[24]

As far as Barrett was concerned, multilateralism had finally triumphed over the unilateralism of the Monroe Doctrine.

In response to direct letters of support, Barrett received replies from President Roosevelt and high Administration officials. The President wrote that he greatly appreciated Barrett's endorsement of the Administration's Good Neighbor Policy of hemispheric interdependence.[25] Secretary Hull expressed concern over Barrett's failing health and acknowledged his contribution to Pan Americanism:

> I have just learned of your protracted illness, and write to express my deep personal interest in your speedy recovery. You have rendered highly

valuable service to the country and to the continent over a long period
of years, and as one thoroughly mindful of this record of yours, I write
to express the earnest hope not only for your speedy recovery, but for
a very long life ahead.[26]

Sumner Welles was especially pleased with Barrett's article on
the Buenos Aires Conference:

I am more than grateful for the work which you have done and which
you are doing in bringing home to our own people the real, concrete
and constructive results obtained from the Buenos Aires Conference.
All of us who are exerting every endeavor to make inter-Americanism
a real and vital force in the interest of the whole continent have every
reason to appreciate your . . . assistance.[27]

Writing from Mexico City, Barrett's old friend Josephus Daniels
took pride in the fact that both he and Barrett had lived to see
the fruition of their long time goals:

Reading last night in the New York *Times* your article about the Buenos
Aires Conference and your lucid presentation of its purposes and achievements, my mind went back through the years of our association. We
are among the few who formed a close friendship during the Cleveland
Administration who have been permitted to live to see many of our
dreams come true.[28]

The article in the New York *Times* referred to by Daniels was
a defense of the Administration's compromise policy at the Buenos
Aires Conference. It was to be Barrett's last publication on Pan
American policy:

The majority of these critics would appear to be under the influence
of that narrow and selfish attitude that the United States must dominate
the other nations of the Western Hemisphere and insist upon its viewpoint
no matter what may be the policies of the other American governments.
It is this position, taken too often in former years by those who do
not understand Pan Americanism . . . and its meaning to the welfare
of the United States, that has seriously interfered with the development
of . . . good will on the part of all Latin America towards the United
States.
    Such critics seem to be indignant and disappointed because President
Roosevelt, Secretary Hull and the United States delegation did not get
all they wanted. They forget completely that the practical success of

any important international conference depends upon the making of reasonable concessions and following a program of justified "give and take." [29]

Barrett never wavered in his support of the Administration's Good Neighbor Policy. In turn Roosevelt welcomed Barrett's endorsement:

I have received with much pleasure your telegram of December 7. I have sent your message to Sumner Welles and I know that he will be happy to receive this expression of commendation from a man who has devoted so large a part of his life to that improvement in inter-American relations which it has been one of the major objectives of this Administration to promote. [30]

This letter was greatly appreciated by the elder statesman, who had recently suffered a heart attack at his home in Coral Gables. Barrett's persistent heart condition would prove fatal to him within a year's time. In the spring of 1938 he suffered another attack. In June he was taken back to Vermont to convalesce. It was there in Bellows Falls that he died on October 17, 1938.

6. Conclusion

THROUGHOUT the course of John Barrett's long diplomatic career, the industrial and technological strength of the United States grew, and the nation rose to great prominence in international affairs. It was in the period 1894 to 1920 that the United States began a vigorous economic penetration of the Far East and Latin America, and in turn assumed a more active political role. This phase of American world involvement reached its climax with the participation of the United States in the First World War.

The elements that contributed to this new role for the United States were forged in the decade of the 1890's and refined in the following decades. The impact of the depression of 1893 convinced politicians, businessmen, and diplomats that the United States would have to seek new opportunities abroad to sustain prosperity and progress at home. Diplomatic and economic policies were joined to form a single powerful thrust toward world power.

In this process a series of reform measures were sponsored by progressive political and diplomatic officials with the support of progressive business interests to achieve this goal. Such measures included: (1) the reorganization of the consular service with appointments based on ability rather than political patronage, (2) government construction of an isthmian canal to facilitate trade with Latin America and the Far East, (3) government subsidies to Pacific steamship lines, (4) a Pacific cable to provide rapid communications

99

for political and economic purposes, (5) the establishment of American branch banks overseas, (6) the permanent exhibition of American products in Asia and Latin America, (7) the training and appointment of commercial attaches in the State Department to promote foreign commerce, (8) the use of organizations such as the American Asiatic Association, and bureaus such as the Pan American Union to collect statistical information and promote foreign trade, (9) American manufacturers were asked to produce goods specifically needed in underdeveloped areas, and to arrange their credit systems with those prevailing in market countries, (10) tariff reciprocity was sponsored to encourage the free flow of trade, and (11) the State Department requested that corporate leaders send engineers and technicians to Latin America and the Far East to work on modern transportation and communication systems, construct electric lighting plants, water works, harbors, and power plants, and develop agricultural, timber, and mineral resources. The United States had embarked upon a systematized progressive program to achieve greatness, and create a stable democratic free-enterprise environment the world over.

The war with Spain, the winning of Caribbean security, and the acquisition of the Philippines gave the United States a fine opportunity to put these measures into action. The State Department subsequently came to view American commerce as an ally in gaining political advantages in the Far East and Latin America. The progressive members of the business community were strongly in favor of this decision. Through such policies as the Open Door and Dollar Diplomacy, a progressive partnership of government and business leadership was formed to create a winning combination for the United States in international relations.

In the midst of these events and policy decisions, the diplomatic career of John Barrett took shape. Although Barrett began his career in an age of imperialism, he was not himself a territorial imperialist. Even prior to the submission of the Open Door Notes by Secretary Hay to the foreign powers in China, Barrett opposed having the United States take part in the political and territorial division of China. The concommitant military and political responsibilities of such division were an unnecessary burden. Instead he wished to safeguard China's independence to insure the availability of trade for American commerce throughout all China's provinces.

In holding this position, Barrett reflected the climate of opinion among American policy makers that led to the issuance of the Open Door Notes. He was not directly responsible for their adoption, but his writings and reports clearly pointed to it as the logical policy for the United States, given its commercial and diplomatic objectives in the Far East. In like manner, Barrett espoused American cooperation with Japan to maintain the Open Door policy in China. Arguing from a position not unlike that of Theodore Roosevelt, Barrett saw in Japan's emulation of western industrial society a commitment to the tenets of the liberal democratic free-enterprise system. Thus Japan appeared to be a natural partner for the United States against Russian and German militaristic imperialism in the Far East.

Barrett reflected the deep sense of confidence in the ability of the United States to develop a modern western-oriented China within the framework of the Open Door Policy. First and foremost the success of this mission rested upon the reconstruction of the Chinese economy. In practical terms this meant creating an American market in China which would eventually result in the adoption of western business methods. Economic prosperity would then lead the way to social and political stability.

Barrett believed that the China market was more than a myth. He was aware that many others considered it to be so because of the lack of Chinese buying power. Barrett, however, felt that the purchasing power of the Chinese could be profitably cultivated if the interior of that nation were opened up through extensive railway construction. With the money received from the sale of raw materials, the Chinese could buy manufactured goods and agricultural products from the United States. Regardless of how basic this answer was, the important point to be made was that the expectation of future gains, and not immediate trade statistics, was what motivated John Barrett to publicize the commercial opportunities of the Far East.

Apart from material economic concerns, a genuine moral attitude was present in American commercial expansion across the Pacific. The United States was fulfilling a civilizing mission in Asia by bringing the benefits of modern industry to underdeveloped peoples. In doing this the United States was part of a progression which began with European colonization in the new world. Barrett believed that the world was evolving toward a higher state of existence. The United States was to be a chosen leader in this evolutionary process in the Far East.

Unfortunately for Barrett, party politics and personal rivalries in the diplomatic corps kept him from continuing his labors in the Asian field. He was able to continue his work as a diplomat and commercial publicist, however, in Latin America. In the capacities of American minister and Director General of the Pan American Union, Barrett contributed to the development of Pan Americanism under Secretary of State Elihu Root. Although it is impossible to state that Barrett was primarily responsible for Root's Pan American policies, it is apparent that he had a definite influence on aspects of their formulation and implementation.

His first step as Director General of the Union was to systematize the statistical resources of the Union into a highly organized body of information. Commercial materials pertaining to Latin American trade was placed at the disposal of all interested parties. Barrett's next step was to expand the duties of the Pan American Union beyond the commercial realm to that of the political. In this way he hoped to achieve political and diplomatic ends without disturbing the blueprint for establishing international peace and progress through mutual commercial interaction.

To this end he sought to have the Pan American Union mediate the Mexican Revolution, Pan Americanize the Monroe Doctrine, and establish the Pan American Union as a hemispheric league of nations. Barrett hoped to replace American unilateralism with a true spirit of cooperation in order to gain the confidence of the Latin American republics. The United States would then be in a better position to work for the creation of responsible democratic governments and viable economies throughout the hemisphere.

But on each of these three issues, the Taft and Wilson Administrations and the State Department decided against Barrett's proposals in favor of solutions that were more narrowly nationalistic. Adverse circumstances also played major roles in keeping Barrett's suggestions from being acted upon. Over the passage of years, however, Barrett's suggestions were eventually adopted in some form.

It was unfortunate that news of Barrett's Mexican mediation offer had been leaked to the press when the United States was attempting its own mediation in San Antonio, Texas. This created a difficult situation among the Mexican factions and resulted in the cancellation of American hopes for peaceful settlement. When the situation further deteriorated, the United States turned to intervention to bring about order in Mexico. This attempt to create political stability by force of arms also failed. Two years later, however, the acceptance of Latin American mediation finally settled the issue, and provided the eventual means for a peaceful solution.

In considering the Pan Americanization of the Monroe Doctrine, the State Department felt this to be a dangerous policy in the years prior to the First World War. The reason was that American national interest was at stake in the economic and political competition with European powers for controlling influence in Latin America. The Monroe Doctrine had to remain a singularly American document.

In future years the Great Depression and narrow economic nationalism would give rise to the Good Neighbor Policy of the Franklin D. Roosevelt Administration as a means of opening up the closed economic and political world order of the 1930's. But in the final analysis, it was the diplomacy of the Second World War which created a hemisphere of politically equal Pan American partners in the cause of common defense. Multilateral defense agreements Pan Americanized the Monroe Doctrine. Thus the United States chose to implement a Pan American policy conceived originally by Barrett in peacetime as a wartime necessity.

Barrett's third innovation, his plan to make the Pan American Union into a regional league of nations, was defeated by Wilson because the President did not want another organization to compete with his own League of Nations. It did not matter that Barrett had been a strong proponent of sanctioned hemispheric cooperation in order to avoid armed conflicts and encourage the expansion of the American political and economic system throughout the hemisphere. The important thing was that Wilson was fighting for adoption of the Versailles Treaty in the United States, and was not disposed to consider any plan which might interfere with his purpose. International cooperation had been a long-standing primary goal of the Wilson Administration. Wilson, however, had his own ideas about how best to achieve it.

But again future developments followed the path outlined by Barrett. In 1948 the Organization of American States was enpowered to mediate its own political conflicts with constitutional authority. Thus each of Barrett's proposals was eventually adopted in some form. Latin American mediation helped to bring a solution to the Mexican Revolution; the Monroe Doctrine was Pan Americanized to protect the hemisphere from external threats and to work toward the creation of a genuine multilateral hemispheric community; and the Organization of American States was endowed with power to deal with political as well as economic issues. Barrett, of course, was not directly responsible for the actual enactment of these measures. But clearly his insight into the course of future Pan American needs and developments provided a model for the consideration of later Pan American policy makers.

This is not to say that Barrett's proposals provided many of the answers to hemispheric problems. Clearly they did not. But they were a necessary evolutionary step toward greater mutual understanding among the American republics. With partial successes, failures, and false starts behind it, the United States in the 1970's will have a genuine opportunity to work toward a true Pan American policy beyond the earlier plans sketched by John Barrett and others. But to accomplish this it will have to be more tolerant of political, social, and economic differences in the hemisphere.

Perhaps the most fitting evaluation of John Barrett's long career as a commercial publicist and diplomat in the Progressive Era was made at the time of his retirement as Director General of the Pan American Union by Secretary of State Bainbridge Colby. On that occasion Colby praised Barrett's work as being essentially that of a missionary. To be sure, Barrett was a missionary for world progress according to the gospel of the American business civilization. He, and others like him, were zealots in the cause of industrial, commercial, and scientific progress.

Notes

PREFACE

[1] Walter Millis, *The Martial Spirit* (Cambridge, Mass.: Riverside Press, 1931), p. 182.

[2] Charles S. Campbell Jr., *Special Business Interests and the Open Door Policy* (New Haven: Yale University Press, 1951), p. 43. Clarence Cary, the New York lawyer and commercial publicist, was one of the largest stockholders in the American China Development Company. John Foord was the secretary of the American Asiatic Association, and an editor of its magazine, *Asia*. He was also an editor of the *New York Journal of Commerce*.

[3] Walter LaFeber, *The New Empire* (Ithaca: Cornell University Press, 1963), pp. 312–313.

[4] Thomas J. McCormick, *China Market: America's Quest for Informal Empire, 1893–1901* (Chicago: Quadrangle, 1967), p. 233.

[5] The first installment of the Barrett Papers was presented to the Library of Congress by the Barrett Family in 1939 and the last in 1958. The collection is divided into five accession groups: 1. No. 11, 625 (42 boxes, 1871–1938), 2. No. 12,830 (4 boxes, 1880–1937), 3. No. G-534 (55 boxes, 1901–1933), 4. No. G-541 (28 boxes, 1885–1938), 5. No. 12,102 (2 boxes of papers belonging to John Barrett's niece, Mary X. Ferguson Barrett). The boxes in each group are in chronological order. Some boxes, although unnumbered, either are dated or have descriptions of their contents on the cover.

[6] Paul S. Reinsch, *Public International Unions* (Boston: Ginn & Co., 1911), p. 145.

[7] Recent revisionist studies that have emphasized the "impact of industrialism thesis" in trying to understand the complexities of the Progressive Era include Samuel P. Hays, *The Response to Industrialism, 1885–1914* (Chicago: Chicago University Press, 1957), and *Conservation and the Gospel of Efficiency: The Progressive Conservation Movement, 1890–1920* (Cambridge: Harvard University Press, 1959); Gabriel Kolko, *The Triumph of Conservatism* (London: Collier-Macmillan Ltd., 1963); Samuel Haber, *Efficiency and Uplift: Scientific Management in the Progressive Era, 1890–1920* (Chicago: Chicago University Press, 1964);

James Weinstein, *The Corporate Ideal in the Liberal State, 1910–1918* (Boston: Beacon Press, 1968); Robert Wiebe, *Businessmen and Reform: A Study of the Progressive Movement* (Cambridge: Harvard University Press, 1962), and *The Search for Order, 1877–1920* (New York: Hill & Wang, 1967); and Jerry Israel, *Progressivism and the Open Door: America and China, 1905–1921* (Pittsburgh: University of Pittsburgh Press, 1971), and "For God, For China and For Yale—The Open Door in Action," *American Historical Review*, LXXV (Feb., 1970), 796–807.

CHAPTER 1.

[1] Mary X. Ferguson Barrett, "The Biography of John Barrett" (unpublished manuscript filed with the John Barrett MSS, Library of Congress, Washington, D.C.), Chapter I, p. 22. All references to the Barrett MSS in this chapter are found in accession group number 11,625 except those of Mary X. Ferguson Barrett which are in no. 12,102.

[2] James G. Blaine, *Twenty Years of Congress, 1861–1881*, 2 Vols. (Norwich, Conn.: Henry Bill Publishing Co., 1884–1886). *Political Discussion: Legislative, Diplomatic and Popular, 1856–1886*, (Norwich, Conn.: Henry Bill Publishing Co., 1887).

[3] David S. Muzzey, *James G. Blaine, A Political Idol of Other Days* (New York: Dodd, Mead & Co., 1934), p. 442f.

[4] John Barrett, "Pan America and Its Inspiration in History," *Records of the Columbia Historical Society* (Washington: Published by the Society, 1916), 157. Also *The Pan American Union: Peace, Friendship, Commerce* (Washington: Government Printing Office, 1911), p. 60. *Bulletin of the Bureau of American Republics* XXX (April-June, 1910), 737.

[5] Mary X. Ferguson Barrett, "The Biography of John Barrett," Barrett MSS, Ch. I, p. 25

[6] *Life and Labors of Henry W. Grady, His Speeches, Writings, etc.* (Atlanta: H. C. Hudgins & Co., 1890), p. 99f.

[7] Raymond B. Nixon, *Henry W. Grady: Spokesman of the New South* (New York: Knopf, 1943), p. 109.

[8] *Life and Labors of Henry W. Grady*, p. 195f.

[9] Albion W. Tourgee, *A Fool's Errand*, (New York: Fords, Howard, and Hulbert, 1879), p. 27.

[10] Barrett wrote to his mother regularly from his first year at Worchester Academy, 1880, until her death in 1926. The closeness of their relationship became especially strong after the death of Barrett's younger sister, Lucy Emily, at the age of eleven months in 1876. At age ten John was again the youngest member of the family. His brother Charles was six years his senior. The correspondence between Barrett and his mother reveals his deep wish to impress her with his accomplishments. This seems especially to be the case after his father's death in 1892.

[11] Mary X. Ferguson Barrett, "The Biography of John Barrett," Barrett MSS. Ch. I, p. 39.

[12] John Barrett to Caroline Barrett, Nov. 25, 1888, Barrett MSS.

[13] Ibid.

[14] John Barrett to his parents, December 16, 1889, Barrett MSS.

[15] John Barrett to Charles Barrett, Dec. 7, 1889, Barrett MSS.

[16] John Barrett to Caroline Barrett, Dec. 25, 1889. Years later Barrett described this period as "'The days of 'Empire'! They could be so defined without exaggeration—those days and years from early 1889–1890, when I was first connected with the *Telegram*, until I left it in early 1894 to go as United States Minister to Siam." Barrett manuscript of an article in the Portland *Evening Telegram* commemorating its 50th anniversary (April 16, 1927), Barrett MSS.

[17] John Barrett to Charles Barrett, Dec. 22, 1889, Barrett MSS.

[18] Barrett manuscript, Portland *Evening Telegram* (April 16, 1927), Barrett MSS.

[19] Ibid.

[20] Ibid.

[21] Ibid.

[22] Ibid.

[23] Martin Fitzgerald (ed.). *Sixty Milestones of Progress, 1895–1919* (Portland: Published by the Ladd and Tilton Bank, 1919). William S. Ladd first arrived in Oregon in 1853. He and Charles E. Tilton were originally merchants who moved with the pioneers to the western frontier. In 1868 Ladd began his first banking venture in Salem, Oregon. The history of Oregon and the history of William S. Ladd were intimately connected. In 1880 Ladd joined forces with Henry Villard, the German-born railroad financier. Villard envisioned a great transcontinental railway with Portland as its western terminus. Villard acquired control of Ladd's Oregon Central Railroad, the Oregon Railway and Navigation Co. and the Oregon Steam and Navigation Co. In 1881 Villard gained control of the Northern Pacific Railroad and combined it with the Oregon roads to create the Oregon and Transcontinental Company. In addition to railway rights, the company was incorporated with the right to establish a steamship line between the Pacific Northwest and China and Japan. Villard and Ladd were well aware that transcontinental rail links were necessary for significant trade expansion beyond the narrow confines of Oregon. The depression of 1883, however, saw this empire fall to pieces. But Ladd withstood the hard times and held on to his financial and industrial interests. The Northern Pacific Railroad and Steamship Company was subsequently completed under the management of Dodwell, Carhill and Company.

[24] Theodore B. Wilcox was president of the Trans-Mississippi Commercial Congress in 1905, and a member of the milling commission of the Food Administration during World War I.

[25] John Barrett to Caroline Barrett, Nov. 18, 1892, Barrett MSS.

[26] See Chapter II for an analysis of Northwestern attitudes concerning overseas trade expansion.

[27] John Barrett to Chauncey F. Black, Sept. 7, 1893, Barrett MSS.

[28] John Barrett to the Acting Secretary of State, Sept. 26, 1893, Barrett MSS.

[29] Theodore B. Wilcox to Joseph N. Dolph, Sept. 16, 1893, U.S. National Archives, *Applications and Recommendations, John Barrett*, Record Group 59, Box 12.

[30] Magnus Crosby to Walter Q. Gresham, Sept. 21, 1893, USNA.

[31] A. Bush to Walter Q. Gresham, Sept. 11, 1893, USNA.

[32] J. J. Kelly, president, Jefferson Democratic Club, to Grover Cleveland, Sept. 7, 1893; Martin Ready, president, Federated Trades Assembly, to Grover Cleveland, Sept. 15, 1893; E. W. Hadley, president, Oregon Pacific Railroad, to John Barrett, Sept. 22, 1893, USNA.

[33] Alex Sweek to Grover Cleveland, Sept. 15, 1893, USNA.

[34] D. R. Murphy, *et al.*, to Josiah Quincy, Sept. 20, 1893; William S. Mason to Grover Cleveland, Oct. 21, 1893, Barrett MSS.

[35] *Ibid.*

[36] Theodore B. Wilcox, *et al.*, to Grover Cleveland, Sept., 1893, USNA.

[37] John Barrett to Peter Studebaker, Oct. 2, 1893, USNA.

[38] Peter Studebaker to Walter Q. Gresham, Oct., 1893, USNA.

[39] Redfield Proctor to John Barrett, Oct. 2, 1893, Barrett MSS.

[40] Barrett manuscript in the Portland *Evening Telegram* (April 16, 1927), Barrett MSS. Some years later Barrett returned Wilcox's favor by endorsing him for a Cabinet post in the Taft Administration. He was unsuccessful, however, in this endeavor. John Barrett to Theodore Roosevelt, Oct. 30, 1908, Barrett MSS.

[41] Josephus Daniels, *Editor in Politics* (Chapel Hill: University of North Carolina Press, 1941), pp. 35–36.

[42] Isaac Townsend Smith to John Barrett, August 30, 1895, May 29, 1896, Feb. 28, 1897, Oct. 29, 1897, Barrett MSS.

[43] Isaac T. Smith to John Barrett, Aug. 30, 1895, Barrett MSS.

[44] This is not to say that John Barrett was directly responsible for the Open Door Notes, nor that he always made recommendations in conformity with their underlying principles. He did suggest, however, the Open Door Policy's basic tenet, that the United States should undertake commercial expansion without territorial acquisition on the mainland of Asia. See Chapter III.

The Open Door principle of equality of trade opportunity in China in fact was employed by the United States throughout the nineteenth century but the term "Open Door Policy" was not used. The treaty of Wanghia, 1844, had incorporated this feature at the request of the Tao Kuang Emperor in order to keep any one power trading in China from gaining a commercial monopoly. See Warren I. Cohen, *America's Response to China*, (New York: John Wiley & Sons, 1971), p. 11.

CHAPTER 2.

[1] See Walter LaFeber, *The New Empire, An Interpretation of American Expansion, 1860–1898* (Ithaca: Cornell University Press, 1963), and Thomas McCormick, *China Market: America's Quest for Informal Empire, 1893–1901* (Chicago: Quadrangle, 1967) for thorough discussions of this development from a revisionist standpoint.

[2] Tacoma *Daily Ledger*, Jan. 6, 1893, p. 1f. Unfortunately Northwestern newspapers in the early 1890's rarely carried the name of the author of an article. This made it impossible to cite with accuracy early newspaper articles written by Barrett from 1890 to 1893.

[3] *Ibid.*, p. 2. The Canadian Pacific Railroad and Steamship Co. was already enjoying subsidies from the Canadian Government.

[4] *Ibid.* As early as 1891 the Seattle *Post-Intelligencer* noted that "The future of Seattle as a commercial port is not a matter of speculation. The completion and operation of competing transcontinental railroads will doubtless bring the establishment of a line of steamships to the Orient and islands of the Pacific." *Post-Intelligencer,* Jan. 1, 1891, p. 1.

[5] U.S. Congress, *Congressional Record* (48th Cong., 1st Sess., Vol. 15; Washington: Government Printing Office, 1885), pp. 150, 1640, 2321, 3639.

[6] Tacoma *Daily Ledger,* Jan. 10, 1893, p. 1.

[7] U.S. Congress, *Congressional Record* (51st Cong., 1st Sess., Vol. 21; Washington: G.P.O., 1890), pp. 382, 1645, 2742, 3807, 4002.

[8] U.S. Congress, *House Reports* (52nd Cong., 2nd Sess., House Report No. 2395) (Washington: G.P.O., 1893), pp. 1–5.

[9] *City of Smokestacks: Everett, the New Manufacturing and Commercial City at the End of the Great Northern Railway on Puget Sound* (Everett, Wash.: Everett Land Co., 1893), pp. 9–10. The Seattle *Post-Intelligencer,* June 30, 1892, p. 4, took comfort in the fact that "as such a commercial center the timber wealth of western Washington yields [to Seattle] magnificent tribute of the millions of foreign gold brought here annually from the great markets of the world by the lumber trade."

[10] Duncan J. Kerr, *The Story of the Great Northern Railway Company and James J. Hill* (Princeton: Princeton University Press, 1939), p. 21f.

[11] U.S. Congress, *Congressional Record* (53rd Cong., 2nd Sess., Vol. 26; Washington: G.P.O., 1894), pp. 6195, 6551.

[12] U.S. Congress, *Senate Documents* (53rd Cong., 2nd Sess., Senate Document No. 53) (Washington: G.P.O., 1895).

[13] *Ibid.*

[14] *Ibid.*

[15] Tacoma *Daily Ledger,* Dec. 6, 1893, p. 4.

[16] Fred H. Harrington, *God, Mammon and the Japanese: Dr. Horace Allen and Korean-American Relations, 1884–1905* (Madison: University of Wisconsin Press, 1944). Harrington's observation that "small men sometimes hold great stakes" is well taken here.

[17] Charles Denby Sr., "The Influence of Missionary Work on Commerce," *The Independent* 53 (Dec., 1901), 2960–2962. Julean Arnold, "Do Missionaries in China Pay?" *Missionary Review of the World* 30 (Fall, 1917), 130.

[18] *Daily Morning Astorian,* Jan. 1, 1890, p. 6.

[19] U.S. Congress, *Congressional Globe* (42nd Cong., 2nd Sess.; Washington: G.P.O., 1873), pp. 303, 870, 2153.

[20] James Blaine Hedges, *Henry Villard and the Railways of the Northwest* (New Haven: Yale University Press, 1930), p. 3.

[21] *Ibid.*, p. 96.

[22] U.S. Congress, *Congressional Record* (46th Cong., 2nd Sess., Vol. 10) (Washington: G.P.O., 1881), pp. 2052, 2966.

[23] U.S. Congress, *Congressional Record* (53rd Cong., 2nd Sess., Vol. 26; Washington: G.P.O., 1894), pp. 1163, 1165.

[24] U.S. Congress, *Congressional Record* (46th Cong., 2nd Sess., Vol. 10; Washington: G.P.O., 1881), p. 2966.

[25] U.S. Congress, *Congressional Record* (47th Cong., 1st Sess., Vol. 13; Washington: G.P.O., 1883), p. 358.

[26] U.S. Congress, *Congressional Record* (52nd Cong., 1st Sess., Vol. 23; Washington: G.P.O., 1893), pp. 181, 1358, 5595, 442, 105.

[27] Tacoma *Daily Ledger*, Feb. 25, 1892, p. 1.

[28] U.S. Congress, *Congressional Record* (53rd Cong., 3rd Sess., Vol. 27; Washington: G.P.O., 1896), p. 1945.

[29] The newspapers surveyed were the Portland *Morning Oregonian*, Portland *Evening Telegram*, *Daily Morning Astorian*, Tacoma *Daily Ledger*, Seattle *Post-Intelligencer*, and San Francisco *Chronicle*.

[30] Cited in Francis B. Loomis, "Foreign Service of the United States," *North American Review* 169 (Sept., 1899), 353. Many noted diplomatic and consular officials started their careers as journalists including Whitelaw Reid, Ambassador to Britain and France and formerly editor of the New York *Tribune*, James G. Blaine, Secretary of State and former editor of the Portland (Maine) *Advertiser*, Francis B. Loomis, Minister to Venezuela and Assistant Secretary of State and former editor of the Cincinnati *Daily Tribune*, Thomas R. Jernigan, Consul-General at Osaka and Shanghai and former editor of the Raleigh (North Carolina) *State Chronicle*, William E. Curtis, first Director of the Bureau of Inter-American Republics and former editor of the *Daily Morning Astorian* (Oregon), and John Barrett.

[31] Seattle *Post-Intelligencer*, April 20, 1890, p. 12.

[32] San Francisco *Chronicle*, July 1, 1893, p. 6.

[33] Tacoma *Daily Ledger*, Nov. 1, 1893, p. 6.

[34] Portland *Morning Oregonian*, Oct. 6, 1893, p. 4.

[35] Lovett M. Wood, ed. of the *Trade Register* (Seattle), to John Barrett, Jan. 25, 1897. Wood praised Barrett for his many articles on behalf of the trade expansion of Puget Sound industries, and the Pacific Northwest. U.S. National Archives, *Miscellaneous Letters to Foreign Consulates, Siam, 1896–1899*, Record Group 84, Box 57–18.

[36] Tacoma *Daily Ledger*, May 31, 1894, p. 4.

[37] *Ibid.*, p. 2.

[38] Tacoma *Daily Ledger*, June 26, 1894, p. 4.

[39] Seattle *Post-Intelligencer*, Aug. 18, 1890, p. 2.

[40] Tacoma *Daily Ledger*, Jan. 6, 1893, p. 2.

[41] Tacoma *Daily Ledger*, July 24, 1892, p. 4.

[42] *Northwestern Miller*, July 24, 1891, p. 1.

[43] *Pacific Lumber Trade Journal*, May, July, Aug., 1900.

[44] *Northwestern Lumberman*, May 1, 1897, p. 2.

[45] *Ibid.* German state paternalism, providing for national direction of overseas commerce, had its roots in the Bismarckian constitution of 1871.

[46] For example see Eric Goldman, *Rendezvous with Destiny* (New York: Knopf, 1952), p. 80f, and David W. Noble, *The Progressive Mind, 1890–1917* (Chicago: Rand McNally, 1970).

[47] Eric Goldman, *Rendezvous with Destiny*, p. 160f.

[48] Daniel Levine, *Varieties of Reform Thought* (Madison: State Historical Society of Wisconsin, 1964), p. 72.

[49] William C. Redfield, *The New Industrial Day* (New York: Century, 1913).

[50] *Ibid.*, p. 75.

[51] *Ibid.*, p. 44.

[52] Charles Ferguson, *The Great News* (New York: Mitchell-Kinnerly, 1915).

[53] *Ibid.*, p. 23.

[54] Edward N. Hurley, *Awakening of Business* (New York: Doubleday, Page & Co., 1917), pp. 104, 208.

[55] Theodore Search, "Developing Foreign Markets," *Northwestern Lumberman* (July 10, 1897), 2.

[56] Albert K. Steigerwalt, *The National Association of Manufacturers, 1895–1914* (Grand Rapids, Michigan: University of Michigan Press, 1964), p. 79. The National Association of Manufacturers was formed in 1895 in Philadelphia. Its organization was originally proposed by the Southern trade journal *Dixie.*

[57] *Ibid.*, p. 79.

[58] *Ibid.*, p. 78.

[59] *Ibid.*, p. 83.

[60] *Ibid.*, p. 86.

[61] *Ibid.*, p. 101.

[62] Jeffrey Safford, "The United States Merchant Marine and American Commercial Expansion, 1860–1920" (New Brunswick, New Jersey: Unpublished Ph.D. dissertation at Rutgers University, 1968).

[63] Albert K. Steigerwalt, *The National Association of Manufacturers*, p. 69. A weak merchant marine law had been passed in 1891 providing subsidies for mail contracts.

[64] *Northwestern Lumberman*, Sept. 2, 1897, p. 3.

[65] *Northwestern Lumberman*, April 9, 1898, p. 3.

[66] *Northwestern Lumberman*, March 13, 1897, p. 3.

[67] *Ibid.*, p. 17.

[68] *Northwestern Lumberman*, Sept. 18, 1897, p. 2.

[69] Samuel Haber, *Efficiency and Uplift: Scientific Management in the Progressive Era, 1890–1920* (Chicago: University of Chicago Press, 1964), p. 99. In a chapter entitled "The Politics of Efficiency," Haber delineates the strong executive, non-partisanship, and the separation of politics from government administration as three major characteristic goals of modern government in the Progressive Era. Haber correctly points to the influence of such men as Frank J. Goodnow and John R. Commons in the development of progressive ideas designed to bring about the existence of a professionally oriented, non-partisan government.

One could also make note of the fact that many progressive era American intellectuals were trained in Germany in the concepts of state paternalism. This was clearly a contributing factor in the evolution of American progressive thought. The most significant German progressive as far as American thought was concerned was Friedrich Naumann, who had introduced a social consciousness into German Progressivism as early as 1890. It was he who advocated the modernization of the industrial state along the lines sketched above.

[70] Walter LaFeber, *The New Empire*, p. 150.

[71] Thomas J. McCormick, *China Market: America's Quest for Informal Empire*, p. 62.

[72] Charles Hoffmann, "The Depression of the Nineties," *Journal of Economic History*, XVI (June, 1956), 153.

[73] *Ibid.*

CHAPTER 3.

[1] John Barrett to Walter Q. Gresham, June 5, 1894, U.S. National Archives, *Despatches from the U.S. Minister to Siam*, Vol. 4, 1894 to 1895, Microcopy No. 172, Roll 4. By the terms of the Franco-British Treaty of 1896, however, the integrity of Siam was guaranteed in order that it might function as a buffer between the French and British colonial empires.

[2] Barrett to Gresham, July 20, 1894, USNA, *Despatches from Siam*, Vol. 4, Roll 4.

[3] Gresham to Barrett, Dec. 13, 1894, USNA, *Diplomatic Instructions of the Dept. of State, Siam*, Vol. 1, 1882–1906, Micro. No. 77, Roll 141.

[4] U.S. Congress, *Papers Relating to the Foreign Relations of the United States* (55th Cong., 2nd Sess. *House Documents* Vol. 1; Washington: G.P.O., 1898), p. 461f. Also see James V. Martin, "A History of the Diplomatic Relations between Siam and the United States, 1833–1929," (Medford, Mass: Unpublished Ph.D. dissertation, Fletcher School of Law and Diplomacy, 1947), 157–200.

[5] Barrett to John Sherman, Nov. 2, 1897, USNA, *Despatches from Siam*, Vol. 7, Roll 7. Dr. Cheek had died during the litigation.

[6] Sherman to Barrett, April 3, 1897, USNA, *Diplomatic Instructions, Siam*, Vol. 1, Roll 141. Barrett was later mentioned as a candidate for Governor of the Philippines on the basis of his success with the Cheek Case. Bangkok *Times Weekly Mail*, Jan. 10, 1899, p. 16.

[7] Siam *Free Press*, Nov. 15, 1897, p. 2.

[8] Barrett to Sherman, April 5, 1897, *Foreign Relations, 1897*, vol. 1, p. 481f.

[9] John Barrett, "America's Interest in Eastern Asia," *North American Review*, 162 (March, 1896), 257–265.

[10] Barrett was tutored in this view by Isaac Townsend Smith, Consul-General for Siam in New York. See above p. 12. Barrett was described as a "convinced advocate of the 'open door!'" Bangkok *Times Weekly Mail*, Jan. 28, 1899, p. 7.

[11] John Barrett, "America's Interest in Eastern Asia," p. 262.

[12] Hermann to Barrett, Jan. 24, 1896, Barrett MSS. All references to the Barrett MSS in this chapter are found in accession group no. 11,625 unless otherwise noted.

[13] Charles H. Dodd to Barrett, March 20, 1897, USNA, *Miscellaneous Letters, Siam*, R.G. 84, Box 51–18.

[14] Theodore Search to John Barrett, Sept. 8, 1896, USNA, *Miscellaneous Letters, Siam*, R.G. 84, Box 51–18.

[15] F. B. Thurber, United States Export Assn., to Barrett, March 7, 1896, Frank Livock, Monarch Bicycle Co., to Barrett, Dec. 11, 1896, E. Wolff, Export Printing and Publishing Co. to Barrett, Dec. 23, 1896, Fred S. Barstow, Hammond Typewriter Co., to Barrett, Dec. 28, 1896, S. S. Gould to Barrett, March 30, 1896, A. E. Cheney, Marion Steam Shovel Co., to Barrett, June 4, 1896, Wolff, Sayer & Heller Sausage Co. to Barrett, June 27, 1896, Empire Moulding Works to Barrett, May 15, 1896, USNA, *Miscellaneous Letters, Siam*, R.G. 84, Box 51–18.

[16] F. M. Smith, Spencer-Clarke Import Co., to Barrett, May 15, 1896, F. L. Zimmerman, Wolff & Zwicker Iron Works, to Barrett, Jan. 23, 1897, W. R. Townshend, San Francisco Bureau of Foreign Commerce, to Barrett, Jan. 17, 1897, A. H. Devers to Barrett, Jan. 26, 1896, Lovett M. Wood to Barrett, Jan. 25, 1897. Barrett received an interesting letter from Arthur L. Adams, an unemployed west coast civil engineer, who, because of the depression, inquired about work directing the "natural progress and development of natural resources" in the Far East. Arthur L. Adams to Barrett, Dec. 10, 1896. USNA, *Miscellaneous Letters, Siam*, R. G. 84, Box 51–18.

During the tenure of Barrett's predecessor in Siam, R. M. Boyd (1892–1893), there were very few requests concerning trade expansion. Barrett's successor, Hamilton King, received a large number of commercial inquiries, but not as many as Barrett.

[17] Hermann to Barrett, Jan. 24, 1896, Barrett MSS.

[18] Hitt to Barrett, June 20, 1896, Barrett MSS.

[19] White to Barrett, May 24, 1896, Barrett MSS.

[20] Receipt of campaign contribution, Barrett MSS.

[21] John Barrett to Caroline Barrett, Nov. 9, 1896, Barrett MSS.

[22] Sherman to Barrett, April 3, 1897, USNA, *Diplomatic Instructions to Siam*, Vol. 1, Roll 141.

[23] Bangkok *Times Weekly Mail*, Feb. 25, 1898, p. 1.

[24] *Ibid.*, p. 2.

[25] Contract between Hearst and Barrett, May 28, 1898, Barrett MSS. Barrett received $700 a month in salary.

[26] John Barrett, *Admiral George Dewey* (New York: Harper, 1899), p. 14.

[27] *Ibid.*, p. 45.

[28] N. B. Scott to Barrett, Aug. 6, 1900, Barrett MSS.

[29] John Barrett, "Imperialism" (1899), Barrett MSS. Barrett gave genuine support to American imperialist arguments in a speech to the New England Society of New York in which he cited an emotional passage from a letter sent to him by General H. W. Lawton, Commander of the Eighth Army Corps in Manila, who had been killed in the Filipino Insurrection. John Barrett to Caroline Barrett, Dec. 14, 1899, Roosevelt to Barrett, Aug. 29, 1900, Barrett MSS.

[30] Bangkok *Times Weekly Mail*, May 27, 1899, p. 7.

[31] *Ibid.*, p. 8.

[32] *Ibid.*, emphasis is mine. Also see Mark Dunnell, "Our Policy in China," *North American Review*, 167 (Oct., 1898), 392–409.

[33] John Barrett, "The Paramount Power of the Pacific," *North American Review*, 169 (July, 1899), 166. Also see Thomas Jernigan, "Commercial Trend of China," *North American Review*, 165 (July, 1897), 63–69.

[34] *Ibid.*, p. 169.

[35] *Ibid.*, p. 171, emphasis is mine.

[36] *Ibid.*, p. 171.

[37] For a recent examination of the commercial aspects of American foreign policy in underdeveloped areas that shows a great deal of continuity with Barrett's interpretation, see Gabriel Kolko, *The Roots of American Foreign Policy* (Boston: Beacon Press, 1969).

[38] See Paul A. Varg, "The Myth of the China Market, 1890–1914," *American Historical Review*, LXXIII (Feb., 1968), 742–758.

[39] John Barrett, "The Paramount Power of the Pacific," pp. 178–179.

[40] See Marilyn Blatt Young, *The Rhetoric of Empire: American China Policy, 1895–1901* (Cambridge: Harvard University Press, 1968), p. 121f. The author states that "Barrett saw no way for America to eliminate the spheres," and "instead of suggesting policies that would halt the trend he advocated joining in the division." This statement simply misinterprets Barrett's intentions. Young's only source for Barrett's thought on the subject is a speech he made to the New York Chamber of Commerce in June, 1899. A more thorough investigation of Barrett's views suggests that Young's interpretation is too limited and thus misleading.

[41] John Barrett, "The Paramount Power of the Pacific," p. 170.

[42] John Barrett, *American Interest in the Far East* (New York: Chamber of Commerce Press, 1899), p. 6.

[43] *Ibid.*, p. 15.

[44] *Ibid.*, p. 18.

[45] John Barrett, "Address before the American Asiatic Association," *Journal of the American Asiatic Association* (Nov. 13, 1899), 64–66.

[46] Barrett listed nine points which would help to realize his objective to expand American trade in Asia: (1) Government construction of the Nicaraguan canal, (2) the laying of the Pacific cable, (3) Government subsidies to Pacific steamship lines, (4) the establishment of American branch banks overseas, (5) the permanent exhibition of American products in China, (6) sending capable businessmen to the Far East, (7) the need for commercial attaches in the State Department, (8) the addition of branches to the American Asiatic Association throughout Asian cities, (9) businessmen themselves should make every effort to search out their own markets in the Far East. *American Interest in the Far East*, p. 15f. Barrett reiterated these proposals when he was transferred to Latin America.

[47] John Barrett, "America in the Pacific," *Forum* XXX (Dec. 1900), 481:

[48] John Barrett, "The Future of Missions in Asia from a Layman's Standpoint," (1899), Barrett MSS. Also see the address by the Rev. E. T. Williams, Secretary of the American Legation in Peking, and later Chief of the Far Eastern Division

of the State Department (1914–1918), on missionaries and merchants in China, *Journal of the American Asiatic Association*, V (March 17, 1900), 88–89.

49 *Ibid.*

50 Extract from speech in support of McKinley, Barrett MSS.

51 John Barrett, "America's Duty in China," *North American Review*, 171 (Aug., 1900), 153, 154.

52 John Barrett, "American in the Pacific," p. 478.

53 *Ibid.*, p. 479.

54 *Ibid.*, p. 479.

55 *Ibid.*, pp. 480, 487. Also see John Barrett, "China: Her History and Development," *National Geographic Magazine*, (June, July, 1901), 269. The Tientsin Treaty concerned trade agreements, extraterritoriality and the opening up of markets in the interior. The Burlingame Treaty dealt with commerce, consular matters and admitted Chinese laborers to the United States.

56 *Ibid.*, p. 483.

57 *Ibid.*, p. 485.

58 North Carolina Bankers' Assn. to McKinley, May 12, 1900, B. I. Wheeler to McKinley, April 18, 1900, A. B. Leonard, Methodist Missionary Society, to McKinley, Sept. 14, 1900, James T. Law to McKinley, April 21, 1900, John Thomson, New York Engineers Club, to McKinley, April 5, 1900, Charles R. Flint to McKinley, 1900, USNA, *Applications and Recommendations*, R.G. 59, Box 12.

59 John Barrett, *Development of American Commerce with China and the Far East, and Its Relation to Our Merchant Marine* (Chicago: National Assn. of Merchants and Travelers, 1901), pp. 5–6.

60 *Ibid.*, pp. 7–8.

61 *Ibid.*, p. 16.

2 John Barrett, "Manchuria—A Bone of International Contention," *Harper's Weekly* (April 20, 1901), 414.

63 See Howard K. Beale, *Theodore Roosevelt and the Rise of America to World Power* (Baltimore: Johns Hopkins Press, 1956), Charles Vevier, *The United States and China, 1906–1913* (New Brunswick, N.J.: Rutgers University Press, 1955), Edward Zabriskie, *American-Russian Rivalry in the Far East* (Philadelphia: University of Pennsylvania Press, 1946), Dana G. Munro, "American Commercial Interests in Manchuria," *The Annals*, XXXIX (Jan., 1912), 154–168.

64 John Barrett, "China: Her History and Development," *National Geographic Magazine* (June, July, 1901), 209–218, 266–272.

65 Portland Chamber of Commerce and Board of Trade to John Mitchell and Joseph Simon, May 28, 1901, USNA, *Applications and Recommendations*, R.G. 59, Box 12.

66 San Francisco Chamber of Commerce to McKinley, May 10, 1901, Los Angeles Chamber to Commerce to McKinley, May 6, 1901, Dallas Commercial Club to McKinley, June 29, 1901, Nashville Chamber of Commerce to McKinley, June 12, 1901, Sacramento Chamber of Commerce to McKinley, May 8, 1901, Tacoma Chamber of Commerce to McKinley, May 31, 1901, Seattle Chamber of Commerce

to McKinley, June 1, 1901, USNA, *Applications and Recommendations*, R.G. 59, Box 12.

[67] Mitchell to McKinley, June 7, 1901, USNA, *Applications and Recommendations*, R.G. 59, Box 12.

[68] Redfield Proctor to McKinley, July 12, 1901, USNA, *Applications and Recommendations*, R.G. 59, Box 12.

[69] Frank Jones to McKinley, May 22, 1901, H. B. Foster to McKinley, June 29, 1901, J. B. Elkins to McKinley, June 15, 1901, Robert R. Hitt to McKinley, May 25, 1901, Charles Grosvenor to McKinley, May 28, 1901, USNA, *Applications and Recommendations*, R.G. 59, Box 12.

[70] Charles Nelson Lumber Co. to McKinley, May 21, 1901, Horace Davis, Sperry Flour Co., to McKinley, May 18, 1901, G.B.M. Harvey to McKinley, June 18, 1901, Daniel A. Tompkins to McKinley, June 11, 1901, Merchants Assn. of New York to McKinley, June 7, 1901, Wakefield Baker, Pacific Coast Jobbers Assn. to McKinley, May 25, 1901, Southern California Fruit Exchange to McKinley, May 8, 1901, USNA, *Applications and Recommendations*, R.G. 59, Box 12.

[71] F. B. Thurber to McKinley, May 29, 1901, USNA, *Applications and Recommendations*, R.G. 59, Box 12.

[72] Board of Foreign Missions of the Presbyterian Church to McKinley, May 14, 1901, USNA, *Applications and Recommendations*, R.G. 59, Box 12.

[73] Paul Varg, *Open Door Diplomat: The Life of W. W. Rockhill* (Urbana: University of Illinois Press, 1952), p. 20.

[74] Fred W. Holls to Barrett, Dec. 12, 1902, Jan. 6, 1903, Barrett MSS.

[75] U.S. Congress, *The Second International Conference of American States* (57th Cong., 1st Sess.; Washington: G.P.O., 1902), p. I.

[76] George B. Lane, "The Role of John Barrett in the Development of the Pan American Union, 1907–1920" (Washington, D.C.: Unpublished Ph.D. dissertation, American University, 1962), p. 140.

[77] *Ibid.*, p. 152.

[78] U.S. Congress, *Final Report of the Louisiana Purchase Exposition Commission* (59th Cong., 1st Sess., Senate Document No. 202) (Washington: G.P.O., 1906).

[79] John Barrett, "The Status of the United States in the Orient," *The Independent* (April 23, 1903), 952–953.

[80] Thomas Hardee, Assistant Secretary of the Louisiana Purchase Exposition to W. B. Stevens, 1903, and Joseph H. Choate, Ambassador to London, to Barrett, Sept. 26, 1902, Barrett MSS.

[81] Portland *Evening Telegram*, May, 1903, p. 24. Barrett's remarks were also designed to encourage a major effort for the success of the Lewis and Clark Exposition to be held in Portland in 1905.

[82] John Hay to Barrett, Dec. 9, 1902, Barrett MSS.

[83] John Hay to Barrett, Dec. 10, 1902, Barrett MSS.

[84] Mitchell to Barrett, Dec. 12, 1902, Barrett MSS.

[85] Holls to Barrett, Dec. 12, 1902, Barrett MSS.

[86] Holls to Barrett, Jan. 6, 1903, Barrett MSS. Holls, Barrett's close friend, warned him that another reason why he was bypassed was that Roosevelt and

some people in the State Department thought he had drawn too much attention to himself with controversial publicity and self-advertisement. Excessive ambition could be a liability as well as an asset.

[87] Barrett to Theodore Roosevelt, July 31, 1905, Barrett to Edwin Wildman, April 2, 1906, Barrett MSS.

[88] John Barrett, "America in the Pacific," p. 483f.

[89] Francis M. Huntington-Wilson, *Memoirs of An Ex-Diplomat* (Boston: Bruce Humphries, 1945), p. 114f.

[90] *Ibid.*

[91] Barrett lecture at Chicago University, Feb. 8, 1901, Barrett MSS.

[92] Barrett to Holls, June 16, 1903, Barrett MSS.

[93] Barrett to Roosevelt, Dec. 30, 1904, USNA, *Applications and Recommendations*, R.G. 59, Box 12.

[94] Barrett to Roosevelt, Dec. 20, 1904, Barrett MSS.

[95] Barrett to the Secretary of State, USNA, *Despatches from the U.S. Minister to Argentina*, Vol. 42, 1903–1904, Microcopy No. M69, Roll 37.

[96] "John Barrett," *The Review of Reviews*, Aug., 1903, p. 143.

[97] "The New Minister to Argentina," *Munsey's Magazine*, Oct., 1903, p. 49.

[98] *National Magazine* (Boston), Sept., 1903, in George Lane, "The Role of John Barrett in the Development of the Pan American Union, 1907–1920," p. 158.

[99] Barrett to the Secretary of State, March 5, and 11, 1904, USNA, *Despatches from Argentina*, Vol. 42, Roll 37.

[100] USNA, *Despatches from the U.S. Minister to Panama*, Vols. 1–3, 1903–1906, Microcopy No. T726, Rolls 1–3.

[101] Barrett to the Secretary of State, July 26, and 27, 1904, USNA, *Despatches from Panama*, Vol. 2, Roll 2.

[102] Barrett to the Secretary of State, Dec. 13, 1904, USNA, *Despatches from Panama*, Vol. 3, Roll 3.

[103] George Lane, "The Role of John Barrett in the Development of the Pan American Union, 1907–1920," p. 167.

[104] Loomis to Barrett, April 29, 1905, USNA, *Diplomatic Instructions of the Dept. of State, Panama*, Vol. 1, 1903–1906, Microcopy No. M77, Roll 126.

[105] George Lane, "The Role of John Barrett in the Development of the Pan American Union, 1907–1920," p. 168. Bowen charged Assistant Secretary of State Francis Loomis with accepting graft while he was Minister to Venezuela.

[106] *Ibid.*, p. 169. New York *Herald*, Sept. 14, 1904, p. 1.

[107] Wildman to Barrett, Feb. 16, 1905, Barrett MSS. Wildman, another close friend of Barrett's, told him that "Some of the men you have been kind to have talked to Taft, [William N.] Cromwell, and Loomis, and left the impression that by your open hospitality and generous assistance you were seeking to appropriate to yourself credit claimed by others and to muzzle them."

[108] Barrett to Hay, Jan. 9, 1905, Barrett MSS. Barrett originally wanted an assignment in Brazil or Mexico.

[109] A committee composed of Nicholas Murray Butler, president of Columbia University, Albert Shaw, editor of *Review of Reviews*, and John Finley, president

of New York City College, was set up to make the awards. Secretary Hay told Barrett that his scholarship plan was an excellent idea, and praised his "undoubted talents and energy." Hay to Barrett, Dec. 29, 1904, Barrett MSS.

[110] USNA, *Despatches from the U.S. Minister to Colombia*, Vols. 62, 63, 1904–1905, Microcopy No. T33, Rolls 62, 63.

[111] George Lane, "The Role of John Barrett in the Development of the Pan American Union, 1907–1920," p. 187. Barrett was particularly concerned about Colombian friendship in relation to the security of the Canal in time of war.

[112] Roosevelt to Barrett, July 15, 1905, Elihu Root to Nicholas Murray Butler, April 19, 1906, Barrett MSS.

[113] Robert Bacon and James B. Scott (eds.), *Latin America and the United States: Addresses of Elihu Root* (Cambridge: Harvard University Press, 1917), pp. 252–253.

[114] Barrett to Elihu Root, Nov. 4, 1905, Root MSS, L.C.

[115] *Ibid.*

[116] Theodore Roosevelt to Barrett, July 15, 1905, Root to butler, April 19, 1906, Barrett MSS. These letters praise Barrett's work. At times, however, there were personal differences owing in large measure to a clash of egoes. Occasionally Barrett tried to share the spotlight with Roosevelt, but the President generally worked alone.

[117] *Speeches Incident to the Visit of Secretary Root to South America*, 1906 (Washington: G.P.O.), P. 266. Also Bacon and Scott (eds.), *Latin America and the United States*, p. 154.

[118] Barrett to Root, Nov. 4, 1905, Root MSS. See above footnote 46, and John Barrett, *American interest in the Far East*, p. 15f.

[119] Barrett to Root, Nov. 17, 1906, Root MSS. Prior to announcing these measures, Barrett noticed that the Secretary had omitted reference to the Portuguese language. Root made the necessary changes, and saved himself the embarrassment of offending Brazil.

[120] Bacon and Scott (eds.), *Latin America and the United States*, p. 254f.

[121] Philip Jessup, *Elihu Root*, (New York: Dodd, Mead & Co., 1938), I, p. 490.

[122] Barrett to Nicholas Murray Butler, Feb. 19, 1906, Barrett MSS. Barrett suggested that the current director of the Bureau, William C. Fox, be transferred to Colombia to make way for Barrett as the new director. When Fox discovered this, he became bitter toward Barrett and plotted against him. Throughout Barrett's tenure as director, 1907–1920, Fox wrote letters to the State Department accusing Barrett of scandalous behavior including the charge that he had turned the Pan American Union Annex into a bawdy house. No credence was given to Fox's accusations. Explanatory letters appear in the manuscripts of Woodrow Wilson, Robert Lansing, Bainbridge Colby, and John Barrett in the Library of Congress.

[123] Elihu Root to Nicholas M. Butler, April 19, 1906, Barrett MSS.

[124] U.S. Congress, *Report of the Delegates of the United States to the Third International Conference of American States* (59th Cong., 2nd Sess., Senate Document No. 365; Washington: G.P.O., 1906), Vol. VI.

[125] George Lane, "The Role of John Barrett in the Development of the Pan

American Union, 1907–1920," pp. 218, 219, 224, 226. The Bureau had been and was to continue to be dependent on the United States. The director was always an American, the Secretary of State was ex officio chairman of the Governing Board, the United States Government controlled its finances, the Governing Board was made up of accredited diplomatic representatives to the United States, and a break with the United States meant a break with the Bureau.

In 1907 when Barrett became director of the Bureau, its staff was twenty-five in number, and its budget was about $60,000 per year. At Barrett's retirement in 1920 the Bureau had a staff of eighty people, and a budget of about $200,000.

[126] U.S. Congress, *Report of the Delegates to the Third International Conference of American States*, p. 43.

[127] E. M. Hood to Barrett, Aug. 2, 1920, Barrett MSS. Hood related Root's opinions in a letter to Barrett upon the occasion of his retirement as Director of the Pan American Union.

[128] John Barrett, "The Land of Tomorrow," *Munsey's Magazine* (June, 1907), 22.

[129] *Ibid.*, p. 36.

[130] John Barrett, "Latin America As A field for United States Capital and Enterprise," *The Bankers' Magazine* (June, 1907), 48.

[131] ———, "Resourceful Central America," *The Review of Reviews*, (July, 1907), 51–65.

[132] ———, "Latin America: A Great Commercial Opportunity," *The World Today* (April, 1908), 67–89.

[133] ———, "A Ready Aid in Foreign Trade," *Systems* (March, 1908), 91–104.

[134] *Ibid.*, p. 93f. Barrett systematized the Bureau into an efficient, progressive organization: "Machinery has been set in motion during the last two weeks to put the Bureau in closer touch, on the one hand, with such organizations as the National Manufacturers' Association, and the National Board of Trade, and, on the other hand, leading universities, colleges and educational institutions." Barrett Memorandum, Jan. 28, 1907, Barrett MSS.

The Independent was so pleased with Barrett's initial efforts that it devoted a special feature to his work: "There is no man in public life today holding a position demanding more vital and able energy, or one so pregnant with possibilities of benefit to the entire hemisphere, yet who is so utterly out of the limelight of popular appreciation and applause as John Barrett, Director of the Bureau of American Republics. . . . There can hardly be a time when John Barrett will be of greater, more vital importance in the hemisphere than now; or such an influence in making the history of the American continent. He is at least in the line for enduring fame." "The Director of the Bureau of American Republics," *The Independent* (Dec. 19, 1907), p. 1500.

Chapter 4.

[1] James G. Blaine, *Political Discussions: Legislative, Diplomatic and Popular, 1856–1886* (Norwich, Conn: Henry Bill Publishing Co., 1887), p. 411.

[2] *Ibid.*, p. 409. Also Alice F. Tyler, *The Foreign Policy of James G. Blaine* (Minneapolis: University of Minnesota Press, 1927), pp. 165–190.

[3] Blaine, *Political Discussions*, p. 401.

[4] Dexter Perkins, *Hands Off: A History of the Monroe Doctrine* (Boston: Little, Brown & Co., 1941), p. 45.

[5] *Ibid.*, pp. 27–64. Also Samuel Flagg Bemis, *The Latin American Policy of the United States* (New York: Harcourt, Brace & Co., 1943), pp. 48–72.

[6] Bemis, *The Latin American Policy of the United States*, pp. 115–125.

[7] Blaine, *Political Discussions*, p. 419.

[8] Allan B. Spetter, "Harrison and Blaine: Foreign Policy, 1889–1893" (New Brunswick, N.J.: Unpublished Ph.D. dissertation, Rutgers University, 1967), p. 195.

[9] Arthur P. Whitaker, *The Western Hemisphere Idea: Its Rise and Decline*, (Ithaca, New York: Cornell University Press, 1954), p. 77.

[10] *Ibid.*, pp. 82–83.

[11] U.S. Congress, *First International Conference of American States* (51st Cong., 1st Sess., Senate Doc. No. 232; Washington: G.P.O., 1890), pp. 225–258.

[12] Alice F. Tyler, *The Foreign Policy of James G. Blaine*, pp. 180–181.

[13] David S. Muzzey, *James G. Blaine, A Political Idol of Other Days*, (New York: Dodd, Mead & Co., 1934), pp. 291, 430f. Also Harold U. Faulkner, *Politics, Reform and Expansion, 1890–1900*, (New York: Harper & Bros., 1959), p. 213: J. Lloyd Mecham, *The United States and Inter-American Security, 1889–1960*, (Austin: University of Texas Press, 1961), p. 50.

[14] Francis M. Huntington-Wilson, *Memoirs of An Ex-Diplomat* (Boston: Bruce Humphries, 1945), p. 252. The intervention of the United States in Nicaragua following the overthrow of Jose Zelaya was enough to instill a new general distrust in Latin America.

[15] George Lane, "The Role of John Barrett in the Development of the Pan American Union, 1907–1920," (Washington, D.C.: Unpublished Ph.D. dissertation, American University, 1962), p. 264.

[16] John Barrett, "Central America's Step Forward," *The Independent* (Jan. 23, 1908), 179–180. Although Washington sponsored the creation of the Court, the United States disregarded its unfavorable decision in a dispute resulting from the Nicaraguan canal-option treaty (1913). The Court eventually collapsed.

[17] Barrett Memorandum, Dec. 4, 1911, Barrett MSS. Some years later Barrett elaborated on his position: "The question of the hour for the United States in the family of nations is this: Shall the Panama Canal, which physically separates North and South America, actually unite them as an everlasting channel of mutual interest and sympathy? No greater disaster could befall the foreign moral standing and commercial opportunity of the United States than to make the Canal purely a selfish instrument of North American material and political activity. We must make our sister republics understand that we want to help them as well as ourselves, that we want to build up their trade as well as our own, that we want their ships as well as those of the United States to utilize its facilities. . . . We must make the Panama Canal a Pan American Canal, and let the opening inaugurate

a new era not alone of material trade and commerce, but of mutual confidence and good will, throughout all the nations that compose the Pan American Union." Barrett address on the Panama Canal, Nov. 9, 1913, Barrett MSS. All references to the Barrett MSS in this chapter are found in accession group no. 11,625 unless otherwise noted.

[18] Barrett address, Dec. 31, 1912, Barrett MSS.

[19] Barrett address, July 20, 1909, Barrett MSS.

[20] During these years Barrett wrote to his mother: "I have confidence in President Taft and believe him to be a man of peace, but I must be frank and say . . . that I think he made a mistake in mobilizing our Army in San Antonio. If he had sent a few regiments to guard the border he would have accomplished the desired results without having at hand that influence for war which is always found in an army anxious for a fight." Barrett to Caroline Barrett, April 19, 1911, Barrett MSS.

On another occasion Barrett remarked: "Both officially and personally, I am doing everything I can in this country to prevent intervention. There are a lot of hotheads who do not stop to think of the awful penalty in our relations with Latin America if we do actually engage in armed intervention. Possibly my judgement is wrong, but my deep interest in our Pan American relations prompts me to think this way." Barrett to Arnold Shanklin, American Consul in Mexico City, Oct. 3, 1912. In a similar manner Barrett noted that, "If the United States should forcibly intervene in Mexico, or engage in an armed invasion of that country without its permission and without justification by international precedents to the satisfaction of its sister American republics, it would strike a self-inflicted and gratuitously staggering blow to its commerce and prestige throughout all Latin America." New York *Herald*, March 12, 1912, p. 3.

[21] Barrett to William H. Taft, Feb. 13, 1913, Barrett to Woodrow Wilson, Feb. 13, 1913, Barrett to Henry Cabot Lodge, *et. al.*, Feb. 13, 1913, Barrett MSS. Officially Barrett acted on his own in making the proposal. He did not submit it to the Governing Board of the Pan American Union for endorsement, although he wrote to President Taft, "I think I can assure you without question that if the plan recommended were adopted it would meet with the unanimous approval of the Latin American countries. . . ."

[22] Barrett wrote to his correspondents that his proposal involved "mediation rather than intervention, international American cooperation rather than individual United States action, and a practical application of the Pan American rather than the Monroe Doctrine. . . . It will be a splendid recognition of the mutual interest of methods akin to international arbitration, and of policies of peace which will unquestionably win the approval of all the world. . . . I have stood from the first, and still stand, emphatically and conscientiously against intervention in Mexico, because I recognize . . . that Mexico's rights as an independent sovereign nation are regarded by the Mexicans and all the other sixty millions of Latin Americans as being just as sacred and inviolate as our own national rights and sovereignty, and that the harm done to the prestige, the good name, influence and commerce of the United States throughout Latin America by unwarranted or hasty intervention

would incalculably and irreparably outweigh any possible good which might result from such intervention." Barrett to Taft, *et al.*, Feb. 13, 1913, Barrett MSS.

[23] New York *Times*, Feb. 14, 1913, p. 1. Four months earlier Barrett wrote that Mexico's "civil struggle has only been going on for half the time that our great Civil War went on. . . . The trouble is that we are impatient and forget the past. If we let Mexico alone she will work out her troubles all right." Barrett to Gutzon Borglum, Nov. 1, 1912, Barrett MSS. Cited in George Lane, "The Role of John Barrett in the Development of the Pan American Union," p. 335.

[24] Barrett to Woodrow Wilson, July 26, 1913, Series 4, Woodrow Wilson MSS. Barrett expanded upon his position in later writings. See *The Pan American Union and Peace* (Washington: G.P.O., 1916), p. 3, and "A Pan American Policy: The Monroe Doctrine Modernized," *The Annals*, LIV (July, 1914), 1–4.

[25] Lloyd Mecham, *The United States and Inter-American Security*, p. 50. David S. Muzzey, *James G. Blaine*, pp. 291, 430f. Harold U. Faulkner, *Politics, Reform and Expansion*, p. 213. Also see Jorge Roa, *Los Estados Unidas y Europa en Hispano America: Interpretacion Politica y economica de la Doctrina Monroe, 1823–1933* (Habana: Carasa, 1935). Helio Lobo, *O Pan-Americanismo eo Brazil*, (Sao Paulo: Eds. da Companhia Ed. Nacional, 1939). Jesus M. Yepres, *Philosophie du Pan Americanisme et Organization de la Paix* (Neuchatel: Eds. de la Baconniere, 1945).

[26] Arthur Whitaker, *The Western Hemisphere Idea*, p. 95f. Dexter Perkins, *Hands Off: A History of the Monroe Doctrine*, P. 247f. Also see F. V. Garcia Anador y Rodriguez, *El Proceso Internacional Panamericano* (Habana: J. Montero, 1942). Carlos Naudon de la Sota, *America Impaciente* (Santiago de Chile: Ed. del Pacifico, 1963).

[27] Whitaker, *The Western Hemisphere Idea*, p. 95. Roosevelt's message was sent to Congress at the beginning of December, 1902; Drago's message was not sent to Washington until the end of the month.

[28] *Ibid.*, p. 102f.

[29] *Ibid.*, p. 106f. Latin American historians and writers have been quick to point this out. See Orestes Ferrara, *El Panamericanismo y la Opinion Europea* (Paris: Le Livre Libre, 1930), and *Tentativas de Intervencion Europea en America* (Habana: Editorial Hermes, 1933); Carlos Pereyra, *La Doctrina de Monroe: el Destino Manifesto y el Imperialismo* (Mejico: Ballesca, 1908); Alberto A. Elmore, *Ensavo sobre la Doctrina de la Internacional* (Lima: Imprento El Comercio, 1896); Carlos Urien, *El Derecho de Intervencion y la Doctrina Monroe* (Buenos Aires: Peuser, 1898); Luis C. Zarate, *La No Intervencion ante el Derecho Americano* (no imprint, 1963).

[30] James M. Callahan, *American Foreign Policy in Mexican Relations* (New York: Macmillan, 1932), pp. 438–439.

[31] Manuel de Oliveira Lima, *Pan Americanismo* (Rio de Janeiro: Garnier, 1907).

[32] Frederic W. Ganzert, "The Baron Do Rio Branco, Joaquim Nabuco and the Growth of Brazilian-American Friendship, 1900–1910," Hispanic American Historical Review, 22 (Aug., 1942), 432–451. Carolina Nabuco, *The Life of Joaquim Nabuco*, trans. Ronald Hilton (Palo Alto: Stanford University Press, 1950),

pp. 288–304. Lawrence Hill, *Diplomatic Relations between the United States and Brazil* (Durham: Duke University Press, 1932), pp. 281–284.

[33] Anibal Maurtua, *La Idea Pan Americana* (Lima: Imprenta La Industria, 1901).

[34] Samuel F. Bemis, *The Latin American Policy of the United States*, p. 194f. Arthur S. Link, *Woodrow Wilson and the Progressive Era, 1910–1917* (New York: Harper & Bros., 1954), p. 105f. Ray Stannard Baker, *Woodrow Wilson, Life and Letters: President, 1913–1914* (Garden City, New York: Doubleday, Doran & Co., 1931), IV, p. 283f.

[35] Perkins, *Hands Off*, pp. 323–324. Also see Santiago Perez Triana, *La Doctrina Drago* (London: Weitheimer, Lea y Cia, no date). In many ways the Drago Doctrine was an official expression of a similar policy put forth by Alejandro Calvo in 1867. See Alejandro Calvo, *Politica Americana* (Buenos Aires: Imprinta La Universidad de J. N. Kingelfuss, 1886), and Alberto Arroyo Rivera, "La no Intervencion in el Derecho Internacional Americano" (Mexico City: Unpublished law thesis, National University of Mexico, 1962).

[36] Donald M. Dozer (ed.), *The Monroe Doctrine: Its Modern Significance* (New York: Knopf, 1965), p. 21. Wilfrid H. Callcott, *The Caribbean Policy of the United States, 1890–1920* (Baltimore: Johns Hopkins University Press, 1942), p. 319, and *The Western Hemisphere: Its Influence on United States Policies to the End of World War II* (Austin: University of Texas Press, 1968).

[37] Peter Calvert, *The Mexican Revolution, 1910–1924: The Diplomacy of Anglo-American Conflict* (Cambridge: Cambridge University Press, 1968), p. 132.

[38] In addition to statements pertaining to the need for constitutional government in Mexico, Wilson adopted the rhetoric of equality when he said of Latin America in Mobile, Alabama "We must prove ourselves their friends and champions upon terms of equality and honor. You cannot be friends upon any other terms than upon the terms of equality. We must show ourselves their friends by comprehending their interest whether it squares with our own interest or not."

The Pan American Pact of 1914, although not ratified, provided for mutual guarantees of territorial integrity and political independence under republican forms of government.

[39] Washington *Post*, July 25, 1913, p. 8.

[40] John Barrett, "A Ready Aid in Foreign Trade," *Systems* (March, 1908), 93.

[41] John Barrett, "A Pan American Policy: The Monroe Doctrine Modernized," *The Annals of the American Academy of Political and Social Science*, LIV (July, 1914), 1–4.

[42] Barrett to Wilson, July 26, 1913, Series 4, Wilson MSS.

[43] John Barrett, "Address on Pan Americanism and the Monroe Doctrine," Speech given before the Illinois State Bar Assn., Feb. 19, 1916, p. 22.

[44] Barrett helped to make arrangements for Wilson's Mobile Speech, and thought himself to have had a direct influence upon its contents: "It would be ridiculous to state that he had not been influenced by things I have said and written and by the work which the Pan American Union has been doing, for to deny that would be a reflection upon this organization, upon myself, and upon his judgement.

Sufficient it is for me that Pan Americanism held the most prominent position in his message." John Barrett to Caroline Barrett, Dec. 11, 1915, Barrett MSS.

[45] *Mexican Herald*, Feb. 14, 1913, p. 3. New Orleans *Item* Feb. 15, 1913, p. 4, Barrett MSS. Panama *Star and Herlad*, Feb. 18, 1913, p. 4. *La Prensa*, Feb. 14, 1913, p. 10, and Feb. 17, 1913, p. 9. In a later issue of *La Prensa* Barrett was spoken of as a champion of Pan Americanism and an official always willing to mediate between the United States and the republics of Latin America, Feb. 25, 1913, p. 10.

[46] *Mexican Herald*, Feb. 14, 1913, p. 3.

[47] New York *Times*, Feb. 14, 1913, p. 2.

[48] New York *Times*, Feb. 16, 1913, p. 2.

[49] *Ibid.*

[50] Barrett to Elihu Root, Feb. 15, 1913: Barrett to William H. Taft, Feb. 15, 1913, Barrett MSS.

[51] Washington *Times*, Feb. 15, 1913, p. 10, Barrett MSS.

[52] *Christian Science Monitor*, Feb. 15, 1913, p. 7.

[53] Detroit *News*, Feb. 17, 1913, p. 4.

[54] New York *World*, Feb. 16, 1913, p. 4.

[55] Editorial, *The Independent*, Feb. 20, 1913, p. 387. "Who Is Responsible?" *The Outlook*, Feb. 22, 1913, p. 394.

[56] Hamilton Holt to Barrett, Feb. 19, 1913; Elihu Root to Barrett, Feb. 17, 1913; J. B. Tait to Barrett, Feb. 15, 1913; Anti-Imperialist League to Barrett, Sept. 15, 1913; Walter H. Page to Barrett, Feb. 24, 1913; Albert Shaw to Barrett, Feb. 24, 1913; L. L. Seaman to Barrett, Feb. 25, 1913; W. P. Massie to Barrett, Feb. 26, 1913; W. Morgan Shuster to Barrett, Feb. 26, 1913; Frank A. Vanderlip to Barrett, March 1, 1913, Barrett MSS.

[57] Salvador Castrillo to Barrett, Feb. 17, 1913; Ignatio Calderon to Barrett, Feb. 17, 1913; F. H. Pezet to Barrett, Feb. 17, 1913; Angel C. Rivas to Barrett, Feb. 15, 1913; Manuel de Oliveira Lima to Barrett, Feb. 15, 1913, Barrett MSS.

[58] Chicago *Tribune*, Feb. 16, 1913, p. 1. John Callan O'Laughlin, the *Tribune's* Washington correspondent, noted that "Mr. Barrett has the backing of the members of the Governing Board of the Union, who would not permit his removal for making a suggestion which would have the effect of placing every Latin American republic on the same plane as the United States in the control of affairs in the western hemisphere." Chicago *Tribune*, Feb. 14, 1914, p. 1.

[59] Heriberto Barron to Barrett, Feb. 14, 1913, Barrett MSS. Barron originally was a follower of General Bernardo Reyes. When Reyes moved to cooperate with Madero in 1911, Barron went over to Madero's side. See Charles C. Cumberland, *Mexican Revolution: Genesis Under Madero* (Austin: University of Texas Press, 1952), pp. 38, 165f.

[60] U.S. Consul Edwards to Secretary of State Bryan, March 7, 1913, U.S. Dept. of State, *Papers Relating to the Foreign Relations of the United States, 1913* (Washington: G.P.O., 1920), p. 759.

[61] New York *Times*, Feb. 15, 1913, p. 2.

[62] Taft to Barrett, Feb. 20, 1913, Series 6, William H. Taft MSS.

[63] Barrett Memorandum, Aug. 22, 1913; Barrett to Joseph Tumulty, Oct. 5, 1913, Series 4, Woodrow Wilson MSS.

[64] Bryan to Wilson, July 19, 1913, William Jennings Bryan MSS.

[65] Barrett to Wilson, July 26 and Aug. 22, 1913, Series 4 Wilson MSS.

[66] Arthur S. Link, *Woodrow Wilson and the Progressive Era*, p. 111.

[67] *Ibid.*, p. 112.

[68] *Ibid.*, p. 113f.

[69] *Ibid.*, p. 116.

[70] *Ibid.*, p. 118.

[71] *Ibid.*, p. 106.

[72] Lansing Memorandum, Dec. 20, 1918, Diary Box 2, Robert Lansing MSS.

[73] Arthur S. Link, *Woodrow Wilson and the Progressive Era*, p. 120. During this period Barrett remarked about Wilson: "He does consult comparatively few persons and does not seem to depend much upon the judgement of those who have had large experience in the lines of his action. Perhaps the best illustration of this is the Mexican situation. There is a general feeling here that he should have avoided some things, which are interpreted as mistakes, if he had listened more readily to the advice of those who thoroughly understood what was going on." John Barrett to Caroline Barrett, Feb. 5, 1914, Barrett MSS.

[74] Link, *Woodrow Wilson and the Progressive Era*, p. 124.

[75] With the announcement of ABC mediation Barrett acclaimed: "Whether the tender of mediation achieves its purpose or not, it has great and far reaching significance. . . . It signifies the true Pan American spirit of getting together among the American nations, and is a long step in advance toward all-American cooperation for the settlement of disputes among the American nations." New York *Times*, April 26, 1914, p. 1.

Although there is no evidence that Barrett was directly responsible for the mediation, the Columbus (Ohio) *Evening Dispatch* stated: "The chances are that if John Barrett's proposition for a Pan-American settlement of the Mexican troubles, made during the Taft Administration, had been accepted instead of rejected . . . we should not now be on the verge of war. . . . Perhaps it would have been different if President Wilson had not come into office with a determination to examine the moral quality of revolutionary governments. . . . things have gone from bad to worse until now the very thing that John Barrett suggested has begun to materialize, and millions of people in this country are hoping that it is not yet too late." Columbus *Evening Dispatch*, May 5, 1914, Barrett MSS.

Robert Bacon also wrote to Barrett "Bully for you and our South American friends! . . . I believe [mediation] to be a great step forward." Bacon to Barrett, April 30, 1914, Barrett MSS.

As a result of unsuccessful attempts that were made to give Barrett credit for the mediation, Barrett wrote to James B. Scott: "In this matter of mediation the whole question is that of achieving peace—who originated the idea is entirely secondary. While what has been done is in absolute accord with my suggestion of over a year ago, which was turned down by the great Huntington-Wilson of the State Department, I would not for a moment think of endangering its success by claiming any credit personally myself." Barrett to Scott, May 9, 1914, Barrett MSS.

[76] Bryan to Messrs. de Gama (Brazil), Naon (Argentina), and Mujice (Chile), April 29, 1914. State Department, *Papers Relating to Foreign Relations, 1914,* Vol. 1, p. 494.

[77] Link, *Woodrow Wilson and the Progressive Era,* p. 126.

[78] *Ibid.*

[79] Edgar E. Robinson and Victor West, *The Foreign Policy of Woodrow Wilson, 1913–1917* (New York: Macmillan, 1917), p. 300.

[80] Lansing Memorandum, June 11, 1914, State Department, *Papers Relating to Foreign Relations, The Lansing Papers, 1914–1920,* Vol. 2, p. 461f.

[81] *Ibid.,* p. 528f.

[82] *Ibid.,* p. 462f.

[83] Lansing Memorandum, Oct. 10, 1915, Diary Box 2, Lansing MSS.

[84] *Ibid.*

[85] In 1916 Barrett volunteered to serve on the joint Mexican-American Commission which was created to negotiate the withdrawal of General Pershing's forces from Mexico. Because Barrett was an international officer, however, he could not participate on such a commission without a special agreement between Mexico and the United States. Barrett to J. W. Belt, Aug. 31, 1916, Barrett MSS.

[86] Elihu Root noted this fact of life at the First Pan American Commercial Conference: "Governments may hold doors open all over the world, but if there is no one to go through them it is an empty form. . . . No Government . . . can make commerce . . . go through open doors." John Barrett (ed.), *Proceedings of the First Pan American Commercial Conference* (Washington: G.P.O., 1911), p. 195.

[87] John Barrett, "Address on Pan Americanism and the Monroe Doctrine," Speech before the Illinois State Bar Assn., Feb. 19, 1916, p. 12.

[88] John Barrett, "The Mighty Meaning of the War for the United States and Pan Americanism," Speech before the Indiana Real Estate Assn., Oct. 17, 1917, Barrett MSS. Barrett made a tour of the war in Europe from September 9 to October 16, 1916 to gather first hand information on the economic impact of the war for Latin America.

[89] John Barrett to Caroline Barrett, Jan. 21, 1911, Barrett MSS.

[90] Other members of the Governing Board included J. P. Morgan Jr., Frank A. Munsey, publisher, Leo S. Rowe, professor of Latin American Studies at the University of Pennsylvania, Assistant Secretary of the Treasury, and chief of the Latin American Division of the State Department, Charles M. Schwab of Bethlehem Steel Corporation, Albert Shaw, editor of the *Review of Reviews,* Frank Vanderlip of National City Bank of New York, Judge James W. Gerard, Melville E. Stone, journalist, financier and president of the Bankers' Club, Archer Huntington, philanthropist, Charles H. Sherill, Minister to Argentina, James Speyer, banker, and E. J. Berwind of the Berwind-White Coal Co. Barrett to Taft, Feb. 19, 1912, Series 6, Taft MSS.

[91] Barrett to Harry E. Bard, Feb. 5, 1917, Barrett MSS.

[92] Barrett Memorandum, Sept. 5, 1920, Barrett MSS.

[93] Barrett was described as the "moving genius" behind the Congress. Washington *Times*, Jan. 3, 1916, Barrett MSS.

[94] *Ibid.*

[95] John Barrett (ed.), *Proceedings of the Second Pan American Scientific Congress* (Washington: G.P.O., 1917).

[96] Barrett Memorandum, Nov. 17, 1917, Barrett MSS. Earlier Barrett had proposed the establishment of a Pan American Food Commission. To this suggestion Bernard M. Baruch optimistically replied: "I know of nothing that will be more helpful than the solidifying of this hemisphere against . . . German influence. The stand taken by the Latin American countries will make Germany realize, before too much blood is shed, that she cannot make headway against a hostile world. Anything that can bring about the better understanding between Latin American countries and ourselves will certainly be mutually advantageous. I certainly agree with your purposes as expressed in your letter of June 2." Bernard Baruch to Barrett, June 4, 1917, Barrett MSS.

[97] Barrett Memorandum, Nov. 17, 1917, Barrett MSS.

[98] Herbert Hoover to Barrett, Nov. 12, 1917, Barrett MSS.

[99] Harry Garfield to Barrett, Dec. 3, 1917, Barrett MSS.

[100] Frank Scott to Barrett, Nov. 22, 1917; George Creel to Barrett, Nov. 20, 1917; Bernard Baruch to Barrett, Nov. 20, 1917; W. S. Clifford to Barrett, Nov. 21, 1917; David F. Houston to Barrett, Nov. 22, 1917; Edward N. Hurley to Barrett, Nov. 23, 1917, Barrett MSS.

[101] Lansing to Barrett, Nov. 30 and Dec. 5, 1917, Barrett MSS. Only eight Latin American countries declared war: Panama, Cuba, Brazil, Nicaragua, Guatemala, Costa Rica, Haiti and Honduras.

[102] Washington *Post*, Nov. 23, 1917, p. 1.

[103] Francisco Yanes, Assistant Director of the Pan American Union, to Barrett, Nov. 23 and 26, 1917, Barrett MSS.

[104] Lansing to Barrett, Nov. 30, 1917, Barrett MSS.

[105] Charles Horner to Barrett, Sept. 3, 1918, Barrett MSS.

[106] The Webb-Pomerene Act permitted American corporations to combine in international trade under government regulation to promote exports. For a reassertion of dollar diplomacy in Latin American see John Barrett (ed.), *Report of the Second Pan American Commercial Conference* (Washington: G.P.O., 1919).

The reentry of the United States into the China consortium is discussed in Paul S. Reinsch, *An American Diplomat in China* (Garden City, New York: Doubleday, Page & Co., 1922), pp. 296–316, 327f, 355f. Also see Benjamin H. Williams, *American Diplomacy, Policies and Practice,* (New York: McGraw-Hill, 1936), pp. 197–198. Roy W. Curry, *Woodrow Wilson and Far Eastern Policy, 1913–1921,* (New York: Bookman Associates, 1957).

[107] John Barrett, "Latin American Trade—A Comparative View," Speech given in 1918, Barrett MSS.

[108] Edward N. Hurley to Barrett, April 6, 1918, Barrett MSS.

[109] Barrett Memorandum, 1920, Barrett MSS.

[110] Barrett to Wilson, Dec. 1918, Series 4, Woodrow Wilson MSS.

[111] Barrett to Wilson, March 4, 1918, Series 4, Woodrow Wilson MSS.

[112] Wilson to Barrett, March 17, 1919, Barrett MSS. Despite Wilson's refusal to accept Barrett's plan he did say that "I can conceive an increasingly useful work lying ahead of the Pan American Union as a means of preserving a perfect understanding between the United States and the American hemisphere."

Barrett also received a letter from Henry Cabot Lodge in which Lodge linked his plan to the preservation of the Monroe Doctrine: "You know what a good opinion I have of the work of the Pan American Union, but I do not feel ready at this moment to discuss what will be the best plan for the preservation of the Monroe Doctrine, which has been a policy of the United States and nothing else." Lodge to Barrett, April 30, 1919, Barrett MSS.

[113] Ann Van Wynen Thomas and A. J. Thomas, *The Organization of American States* (Dalles: Southern Methodist University Press, 1963), p. 416. After 1948 the Pan American Union became the General Secretariat of the Organization of American States.

[114] New York *Times*, April 4, 1919, p. 1.

[115] John Barrett to Caroline Barrett, Oct. 1, 1919; Barrett to Francis Loomis, March 6, 1920, Barrett MSS.

[116] David E. Cronin (ed.), *The Cabinet Diaries of Josephus Daniels* (Lincoln: University of Nebraska Press, 1963). William McAdoo to Woodrow Wilson, Jan. 3, 1917, McAdoo MSS.

[117] Bainbridge Colby to Wilson, April 28, 1920, Bainbridge Colby MSS.

[118] George Lane, "The Role of John Barrett in the Development of the Pan American Union, 1907–1920," p. 524.

[119] Francisco Yanes to Barrett, Nov. 26, 1917, Barrett MSS.

[120] George Lane, "The Role of John Barrett in the Development of the Pan American Union, 1907–1920," p. 526.

[121] *Ibid.* Ignacio Calderon of Bolivia led the drive against Barrett.

[122] Mary X. Ferguson Barrett, "The Biography of John Barrett" (Unpublished manuscript filed with the John Barrett MSS, Library of Congress, Washington, D. C.), Ch. X, p. 30.

[123] George M. Cornwall to Barrett, Jan. 31, 1919, Barrett MSS, accession no. G-534.

[124] Charles Schnabel to Barrett, Aug. 7, 1920, Barrett MSS, G-534.

[125] H. Daniels to Barrett, Aug. 4, 1920, Barrett MSS, G-534.

[126] Arthur Bullard to Barrett, Sept. 9, 1920; A. F. DuPont to Barrett, July 14, 1919; Aubrey Drury, World Trade Club, to Barrett, March 12, 1920, Barrett MSS. The Barrett MSS contain many letters of praise and support from commercial and diplomatic interests for the entire period of Barrett's tenure as Director General, G-534.

[127] Homer Brett to Barrett, Sept. 29, 1920, Barrett MSS.

CHAPTER 5.

[1] George Lane, "The Role of John Barrett in the Development of the Pan

American Union, 1907–1920," p. 516. I have used Lane as a guide to this last segment of Barrett's life along with Mary X. Ferguson Barrett, "The Biography of John Barrett," Ch. X.

[2] Barrett manuscript of an article for *El Universal* (1921), Barrett MSS. All references in this chapter to the Barrett MSS are found in accession group no. 11,625. Also see Barrett's letterbooks in group no. 12,830.

[3] George F. Summerlin, Charge, Mexico City, to Henry P. Fletcher, Dec. 2, 1921, U.S. Dept. of State, *Records of the State Dept. Relating to Political Relations between the United States and Mexico, 1910–1929,* R.G. 59, Microcopy No. 314, Roll 20. In an article for *El Universal* Barrett was especially critical of the fact that without formal relations between Mexico and the United States, Mexico was denied a seat on the Governing Board of the Pan American Union. Barrett manuscript of article, *El Universal,* Dec. 21, 1921, Barrett MSS.

[4] Mary X. Ferguson Barrett, "The Biography of John Barrett," Ch. X, p. 37.

[5] Barrett to Warren Harding, Feb. 10, 1921, Barrett MSS.

[6] *Ibid.*

[7] Barrett to Charles Evans Hughes, Nov. 11, 1923. Barrett MSS.

[8] Francis White to Charles Evans Hughes, Sept. 26, 1924, cited in Lane, "The Role of John Barrett in the Development of the Pan AmericanUnion," p. 549.

[9] *Ibid.*, p. 551. See the New York *Times,* May 10, 1926, p. 4.

[10] Everett Saunders, Coolidge's Secretary to Barrett, April 13, 1927, Barrett to John H. Hammond, July 16, 1927, Barrett to William Borah, *et. al.*, Sept. 30, 1927, Barrett MSS.

[11] The fact that Barrett attacked one of the State Department's own, Leo S. Rowe, his successor as Director-General, in his letter was exactly the sort of thing which hindered Barrett's chances for diplomatic appointment.

[12] George Akerson, Asst. to the President-elect, to Barrett, Jan. 17, 1929, Barrett MSS.

[13] Barrett to Frederick Allen, Oct. 9, 1930, Barrett MSS.

[14] New York *Times,* June 4, 1931, editorial page.

[15] New York *Times,* Aug. 19, 1931, Barrett MSS. The *Times* did not publish the letter.

[16] New York *Herald-Tribune,* Aug. 7, 1932, editorial page.

[17] New York *Times,* Nov. 20, 1932, editorial page.

[18] Barrett to Franklin D. Roosevelt, April 8, 1933, Barrett MSS.

[19] Barrett to Roosevelt, Sept. 26, 1933, Barrett MSS.

[20] Barrett to Roosevelt, Oct. 13, 1933, Barrett MSS. When Barrett began writing to Roosevelt, he eased his criticism in the press. Because of failing health he retired to Coral Gables, Florida in 1930. During this time he was appointed to the Advisory Council of the Institute of Inter-American Affairs at the University of Florida, and conducted a lecture series in May, 1933 at Rollins College.

[21] Sumner Welles to Barrett, May 23, 1933; Cordell Hull to Barrett, Jan. 22, 1934, Barrett MSS.

[22] Hull to Barrett, Jan. 22, 1934, Barrett MSS.

[23] Mary X. Ferguson Barrett, "The Biography of John Barrett," Ch. X, p. 61.

[24] John Barrett, "President Roosevelt's Plan for a Pan American Peace Conference," Address before the Pan American League of Miami, Feb. 25, 1936, Barrett MSS.

[25] Roosevelt to Barrett, Dec. 11, 1936, Barrett MSS.

[26] Hull to Barrett, Feb. 21, 1937, Barrett MSS.

[27] Sumner Welles to Barrett, Jan. 25, 1937, Barrett MSS.

[28] Josephus Daniels to Barrett, Feb. 2, 1937, Barrett MSS.

[29] New York *Times*, Jan. 24, 1937, p. 4.

[30] Roosevelt to Barrett, Dec. 15, 1937, Barrett MSS.

Bibliography

PRIMARY SOURCES

Manuscripts in the Library of Congress, Washington, D. C.
Barrett, John, MSS.
Bryan, William Jennings, MSS.
Cleveland, Grover, MSS.
Colby, Bainbridge, MSS.
Griscom, Lloyd C., MSS.
Hay, John Milton, MSS.
Knox, Philander C., MSS.
Lansing, Robert, MSS.
McKinley, William, MSS.
Olney, Richard, MSS.
Roosevelt, Theodore, MSS.
Root, Elihu, MSS.
Sherman, John, MSS.
Taft, William Howard, MSS.
Wilson, Woodrow, MSS.

Public Documents

Barrett, John (ed.), *Proceedings of the First Pan American Commercial Conference.* Washington: Government Printing Office, 1911.
————. *Proceedings of the Second Pan American Commercial Conference.* Washington: G.P.O., 1919.
————. *Proceedings of the Second Pan American Scientific Congress.* Washington: G.P.O., 1917.
U.S. Congress, *Congressional Globe, 1859–1873.* Washington: G.P.O., 1859–1873.
————, *Congressional Record, 1873–1920.* Washington: G.P.O., 1873–1920.
————, *Final Report of the Louisiana Purchase Exposition Commission.* (59th Cong., 1st Sess., Senate Document No. 202.) Washington: G.P.O., 1906.

_____, *First International Conference of American States*. (51st Cong., 1st Sess., Senate Document No. 232.) Washington: G.P.O., 1890.

_____, *Papers Relating to the Committee on Interstate and Foreign Commerce.* (52nd Cong., 2nd Sess., Vol. 2.) Washington: G.P.O., 1893.

_____, *Papers Relating to the Foreign Relations of the United States, 1898.* (55th Cong., 2nd Sess.. Vol. 1.) Washington: G.P.O., 1899.

_____, *Papers Relating to the Foreign Relations of the United States, 1905.* (59th Cong., 1st Sess., Vol. 1.) Washington: G.P.O., 1906.

_____, *Papers Relating to the Foreign Relations of the United States, 1906.* (59th Cong., 2nd Sess., Vol. 1, Part 1.) Washington: G.P.O., 1907.

_____, *Papers Relating to the Foreign Relations of the United States, 1906.* (59th Cong., 2nd Sess., Senate Document No. 211.) Washington: G.P.O., 1909.

_____, *Second International Conference of American States*. (57th Cong., 1st Sess., Senate Report No. 330.) Washington: G.P.O., 1902.

_____, *Third International Conference of American States*. (59th Cong., 2nd Sess., Senate Document No. 365.) Washington: G.P.O., 1906.

U.S. Dept. of State, *Papers Relating to the Foreign Relations of the United States, 1913.* Washington: G.P.O., 1920.

_____, *Papers Relating to the Foreign Relations of the United States, 1914.* Washington: G.P.O., 1922.

_____, *Papers Relating to the Foreign Relations of the United States. The Lansing Papers, 1914–1920.* 2 vols. Washington: G.P.O., 1944.

_____, *Records of the State Department Relating to Political Relations between the United States and Mexico, 1910–1929.* R.G. 59, Microcopy No. 314, Roll 20.

U.S. National Archives, *Applications and Recommendations, John Barrett*, R. G. 59, Box 12.

_____, *Despatches from the U.S. Minister to Argentina.* Vols. 41–42, Aug., 1902–Nov., 1903, Aug. 1903–June, 1904, Microcopy No. 69, Rolls 36, 37.

_____, *Despatches from the U.S. Minister to Colombia.* Vols. 62–63, May, 1904–Feb., 1905, March, 1905–Dec., 1905, Microcopy No. T33, Rolls 62, 63.

_____, *Despatches from the U.S. Minister to Panama.* Vols. 1–3, Dec., 1903–Feb., 1904, Feb.–Aug., 1904, Sept., 1904–April, 1905, Microcopy No. T726, Rolls 1–3.

_____, *Despatches from the U.S. Minister to Siam.* Vol. 4, April, 1894–Feb., 1898, Microcopy No. 172, Rolls 4–7.

_____, *Diplomatic Instructions of the Department of State, Argentina.* Vols. 17–18, Jan., 1892–Aug., 1906, Microcopy No. 77, Roll 12.

_____, *Diplomatic Instructions of the Department of State, Colombia.* Vol. 19, Nov., 1898–Aug., 1906, Microcopy No. 77, Roll 48.

_____, *Diplomatic Instructions of the Department of State, Panama.* Vol. 1, Dec. 1903–Aug., 1906, Microcopy No. 77, Roll 126.

_____, *Diplomatic Instructions of the Department of State, Siam.* Vol. 1, Aug., 1882–Aug., 1906, Microcopy No. 77, Roll 141.

————, *Miscellaneous Letters, Siam, 1896–1899*, R. G. 84, Box 57–18.

Books

Bacon, Robert and James B. Scott (eds.). *Latin America and the United States: Addresses by Elihu Root.* Cambridge: Harvard University Press, 1917.

Barrett, John. *Admiral George Dewey.* New York: Harper, 1899.

————. *Mexico: A Review and a Forecast.* Washington: G.P.O., 1917.

————. *The Call of South America.* New York: Pan American Society Press, 1922.

————. *The Panama Canal—What It is, What It Means.* Washington: Pan American Union Press, 1914.

————. *The Pan American Union and Peace.* Washington: G.P.O., 1916.

————. *The Pan American Union: Peace, Friendship, Commerce.* Washington: G.P.O., 1911.

Blaine, James G. *Political Discussions: Legislative, Diplomatic, and Popular, 1856–1886.* Norwich, Conn.: The Henry Bill Co., 1887.

————. *Twenty Years of Congress, 1861–1881.* 2 vols. Norwich, Conn.: The Henry Bill Co., 1884, 1886.

Calvo, Alejandro. *Politica Americana.* Buenos Aires: Imprinta La Universidad de J. N. Kingelfuss, 1896.

City of Smokestacks: Everett, the New Manufacturing and Commercial City at the End of the Great Northern Railway on Puget Sound. Everett, Washington: Everett Land Co., 1893.

Daniels, Josephus. *Editor in Politics.* Chapel Hill: University of North Carolina Press, 1941.

Ferguson, Charles. *The Great News.* New York: Mitchell-Kinnerly, 1915.

Grady, Henry Woodfin. *The New South.* New York: Robert Bonner's Sons, 1890.

Griscom, Lloyd C. *Diplomatically Speaking.* Boston: Little, Brown & Co., 1940.

Holls, Frederick W. *The Peace Conference at the Hague.* New York: Macmillan, 1900.

Huntington-Wilson, Francis M. *Memoirs of An Ex-Diplomat.* Boston: Bruce-Humphries, 1945.

Hurley, Edward N. *Awakening of Business.* New York: Doubleday, Page & Co., 1917.

Kelley, William D. *The Old South and the New South.* New York: G. P. Putnam's Sons, 1888.

Life and Labors of Henry W. Grady, His Speeches, Writings, Etc. Atlanta: H. C. Hudgins & Co., 1890.

McAdoo, William G. *Crowded Years.* Boston: Houghton Mifflin Co., 1931.

Perez Triana, Santiago. *La Doctrina Drago.* London: Weithemer, Lea y Cia, no date.

Redfield, William C. *The New Industrial Day.* New York: Century, 1913.

Reinsch, Paul S. *An American Diplomat in China.* Garden City, New York: Doubleday, Page & Co., 1922.

————. *Public International Unions.* Boston: Ginn & Co., 1911.

Speeches Incident to the Visit of Secretary Root to South America, 1906. Washington: G.P.O., 1906.

Tompkins, Daniel A. *American Commerce: Its Expansion.* Charlotte, No. Carolina: Published by the author, 1900.

_____. *National Expansion.* Charlotte, No. Carolina: Published by the author, 1899.

Tourgee, Albion W. *A Fool's Errand.* New York: Fords, Howard and Hulbert, 1879.

Vanderlip, Frank A. *The American Commercial Invasion of Europe.* New York: Charles Scribner's Sons, 1902.

Villard, Henry. *Memoirs of Henry Villard.* 2 vols. Boston: Houghton Mifflin Co., 1904.

_____. *The Early History of Transportation in Oregon.* Eugene: University of Oregon Press, 1944.

Wells, David A. *The Question of Ships.* New York: G. P. Putnam's Sons, 1890.

Articles

Arnold, Julean. "Do Missionaries in China Pay?" *Missionary Review of the World,* 30 (Fall, 1917), 130.

Barrett, John. "A Pan American Policy: The Monroe Doctrine Modernized," *The Annals of the American Academy of Political and Social Science,* LIV (July, 1914), 1–4.

_____. "A Ready Aid in Foreign Trade," *Systems* (March, 1908), 91–104.

_____. "America in China: Our Position and Opportunity," *North American Review,* 175 (1902), 655–663.

_____. "America in the Pacific," *Forum,* XXX (Dec., 1900), 478–491.

_____. "America in the Pacific and Far East," *Harper's Monthly,* 99 (Nov., 1899), 917–926.

_____. "America's Duty in China," *North American Review,* 171 (Aug., 1900), 145–157.

_____. "America's Interest in Eastern Asia," *North American Review,* 162 (March, 1896), 257–265.

_____. "Central America's Step Forward," *The Independent,* 64 (Jan. 23, 1908), 179–180.

_____. "China: Her History and Development," *National Geographic Magazine* (June–July, 1901), 209–218, 266–272.

_____. "Cuba of the Far East," *North American Review,* 164 (Feb., 1899), 173–180.

_____. "The Land of Tomorrow," *Munsey's Magazine* (June, 1907), 21–36.

_____. "Latin America: A Great Commercial Opportunity," *The World Today* (April, 1908), 67–89.

_____. "Latin America as a Field for United States Capital and Enterprise," *The Bankers' Magazine* (June, 1907), 38–49.

Barrett, John. "Manchuria—A Bone of International Contention," *Harper's Weekly* (April 20, 1901), 414.

————. "The New Japan," *Review of Reviews*, 26 (Dec., 1902), 694–696.

————. "The New Pan Americanism," *Everybody's Magazine*, 41 (July, 1919), 78–88.

————. "Our Merchant Marine and the South American Republics," *Scientific America*, 105 (July 15, 1911), 48–49.

————. "Pan American Outlook," *Journal of Race Development*, 9 (Oct., 1918), 114–119.

————. "Pan American Possibilities," in *Latin America*, George Blakeslee ed. New York: Stechert, 1914, 19–29.

————. "The Pan American Union and the inventor," *Scientific America*, 104 (March 4, 1911), 232–234.

————. "Pan Americanism and Its Inspiration in History," *Records of the Columbia Historical Society* (1916), 156–159.

————. "The Paramount Power of the Pacific," *North American Review*, 169 (July, 1899), 165–179.

————. "The Philippines: Our Approach to Asia," *Harper's Weekly* (July 28, 1900), 702–703.

————. "The Plain Truth about Asiatic Labor," *North American Review*, 162 (Nov., 1896), 620–632.

————. "Political Possibilities in China," *Harper's Weekly* (July 7, 1900), 619.

————. "Practical Pan Americanism," *North American Review*, 202 (Sept., 1915), 145–153.

Barrett, John and Hugh Lusk. "The Problem of the Philippines," *North American Review*, 167 (Sept., 1898), 257–277.

Barrett, John. "Resourceful Central America," *Review of Reviews* (July, 1907), 51–65.

————. "Siam, a Remarkable Kingdom of Asia," *The Vermonter*, VIII (Aug., 1902), 20–25.

————. "The Status of the United States in the Orient," *The Independent*, (April 23, 1903), 952–953.

————. "The United States and Latin America," *North American Review*, 183 (Sept., 1906), 474–483.

————. "W. W. Rockhill: An Appreciation," *The Independent*, (Oct. 31, 1901), 2564–2565.

————. "The War and the New America—The New Pan America," *The World Court*, 3 (Nov., 1917), 564–565.

————. "What America Has at Stake in China," *Harper's Weekly* (Aug. 11, 1900), 745.

————. "What the War Has Done to the Monroe Doctrine," *Current Opinions*, 65 (Nov., 1918), 291–293.

Calderon, Ignacio. "Pan American Ideals and the War," *Journal of Race Development*, 9 (Oct., 1918), 190–213.

————. "The Pan American Union and the Monroe Doctrine," *Journal of International Relations*, 10 (Oct., 1919), 133–137.

Denby Sr., Charles. "The Influence of Missionary Work on Commerce," *The Independent*, 53 (Dec., 1901), 2960–2962.

Dunnell, Mark. "Our Policy in China," *North American Review*, 167 (Oct., 1898), 392–409.

Editorial. "John Barrett," *Review of Reviews* (Aug., 1903), 143.

Editorial. "The New Minister to Argentina," *Munsey's Magazine* (Oct., 1903), 49.

Jerrigan, Thomas. "Commercial Trends of China," *North American Review*, 165 (July, 1897), 63–69.

Loomis, Francis B. "The Foreign Service of the United States," *North American Review*, 169 (Sept., 1899), 349–361.

Search, Theodore. "Developing Foreign Markets," *Northwestern Lumberman* (July 10, 1897), 2–4.

Williams, Edward T. "Missionaries and Merchants in China," *Journal of the American Asiatic Association*, V (March 17, 1900), 88–89.

Wilson, Woodrow. "The Deeper Union of the Americas," *Journal of American History*, 8 (1914), 460–464.

Addresses and Speeches

Barrett, John. "Address," Speech given before the American Asiatic Association, Nov. 13, 1899.

————. "America and Asia: A Survey of Present Critical Conditions in the trade of the United States with the Far East," Address before the trans-Mississippi Congress in Portland, Oregon, Aug. 17, 1905.

————. "American Interests in the Far East," Delivered to the New York State Chamber of Commerce, June 1, 1899.

————. "Development of American Commerce with China and the Far East, and Its Relation to Our Merchant Marine," Address before the National Association of Merchants and Travelers, Chicago, Feb. 5, 1901.

————. "The Future of Missions in Asia from a Layman's Standpoint," Address given in 1899, Barrett MSS.

————. "The Latin American Field and Opportunity," Address before the National Education Association, Washington, 1915.

————. "The Mighty Meaning of the War for the United States, and Pan Americanism," Speech before the Indiana Real Estate Association, South Bend, Oct. 17, 1917.

————. "Pan Americanism and the Monroe Doctrine," Speech before the Illinois State Bar Association, Chicago, Feb. 16, 1916.

————. "President Roosevelt's Plan for a Pan American Peace Conference," Address before the Pan American League of Miami, Feb. 25, 1936.

Newspapers

Bangkok *Times Weekly Mail*, 1898–1899.

Chicago *Tribune*, 1913.

Daily Morning Astorian, 1890–1891.

La Prensa (Buenos Aires), Feb., 1913.

New York *Times*, 1913–1938.

Panama *Star and Herald*, Feb., 1913.

Portland *Evening Telegram*, 1881–1883, 1887, 1900–1903.
Portland *Morning Oregonian*, 1892–1894.
San Francisco *Chronicle*, 1892–1894.
Seattle *Post-Intelligencer*, 1890–1892.
Siam *Free Press*, Nov., 1897.
Tacoma *Daily Ledger*, 1891–1895.
Washington *Post*, 1913–1920.

Trade Journals

Journal of the American Asiatic Association, 1898–1902.
Pacific Lumber Trade Journal, 1899–1907.
Pacific Marine Review, 1907–1912.
Northwestern Lumberman, 1897–1898.
Northwestern Miller, 1891.
Southern Lumberman, 1899–1901.
The Timberman, 1909.
West Coast Lumberman, 1913.
West Coast Trade, 1892.

Secondary Sources

Anador, F. V. Garcia y Rodriguez. *El Proceso Internacional Panamericano.* Habana: J. Montero, 1942.

Baker, Ray Stannard. *Woodrow Wilson, Life and Letters: President. 1913–1914.* Garden City, New York: Doubleday, Doran & Co., 1931.

Bancroft, Hubert Howe. *The New Pacific.* New York: The Bancroft Co., 1900.

Barrett, Mary X. Ferguson. "The Biography of John Barrett," Unpublished manuscript in the John Barrett MSS, Library of Congress.

Beale, Howard K. *Theodore Roosevelt and the Rise of America to World Power.* Baltimore: Johns Hopkins Press, 1956.

Bemis, Samuel Flagg. *The American Secretaries of State and Their Diplomacy.* New York: Knopf, 1928.

———. *The Latin American Policy of the United States.* New York: Harcourt, Brace & Co., 1943.

Bernstein, Barton J. and F. A. Leib. "Progressive Republican Senators and American Imperialism, 1898–1916: A Reappraisal," *Mid-America,* L (Sept., 1968), 163–205.

Bingham, Hiram. *The Monroe Doctrine: An Obsolete Shibboleth.* New Haven: Yale University Press, 1913.

Blakeslee, George H. "True Pan-Americanism: A Policy of Cooperation with the Other American Republics," *Journal of Race Development,* 7 (Jan. 1917), 342–360.

Bolton, Herbert E. and H. Morse Stephens (eds.). *The Pacific Ocean in History: Papers and Addresses Presented at the Panama-Pacific Historical Congress, 1915.* New York: Macmillan, 1917.

Bonsal, Stephen. *The American Mediterranean*. New York: Moffat, Yard & Co., 1913.

Calero, Manuel. *The Mexican Policy of President Woodrow Wilson as It Appears to a Mexican*. New York: Smith & Thomson, 1916.

Callahan, James Morton. *American Foreign Policy in Mexican Relations*. New York: Macmillan, 1932.

Callcott, Wilfrid H. *The Caribbean Policy of the United States, 1890–1920*. Baltimore: Johns Hopkins Press, 1942.

_____. *The Western Hemisphere: Its Influence on United States Policies to the End of World War II*. Austin: University of Texas Press, 1968.

Calvert, Peter. *The Mexican Revolution, 1910–1914: The Diplomacy of Anglo-American Conflict*. Cambridge: Cambridge University Press, 1968.

Campbell, Charles S. *Special Business Interests and the Open Door Policy*. New Haven: Yale University Press, 1951.

Campbell, E. G. *The Reorganization of the American Railroad System, 1893–1900*. New York: Columbia University Press, 1938.

Cassey, John W. "The Mission of Charles Denby Sr. and International Rivalries in the Far East, 1885–1898," Los Angeles: Unpublished Ph.D. dissertation, University of Southern California, 1959.

Casey, Clifford B. "The Creation and Development of the Pan American Union," *Hispanic American Historical Review*, 13 (Nov., 1933), 437–456.

Cline, Howard F. *The United States and Mexico*. Cambridge: Harvard University Press, 1953.

Chambers, Clark A. "The Belief in Progress in Twentieth Century America," *Journal of the History of Ideas*, XIX (April, 1958), 197–224.

Cohen, Warren I. *America's Response To China* New York: John Wiley and Sons, 1971.

Cooper, John Milton. "Progressivism and American Foreign Policy: A Reconsideration," *Mid-America*, 51 (Oct., 1969), 260–277.

Croly, Herbert. *Willard Straight*. New York: Macmillan, 1924.

_____. *The Promise of American Life*. New York: Macmillan, 1909.

Cronin, David E. (ed.). *The Cabinet Diaries of Josephus Daniels*. Lincoln: University of Nebraska Press, 1963.

Cumberland, Charles C. *Mexican Revolution: Genesis Under Madero*. Austin: University of Texas Press, 1952.

Curry, Roy W. *Woodrow Wilson and Far Eastern Policy, 1913–1921*. New York: Bookman Associates, 1957.

Dozer, Donald M. (ed.). *The Monroe Doctrine: Its Modern Significance*. New York: Knopf, 1965.

Elmore, Alberto A. *Ensayo sobre la Doctrina de la Internacional*. Lima: Imprento El Comercio, 1896.

Faulkner, Harold U. *Politics, Reform and Expansion, 1890–1900*. New York: Harper & Bros., 1959.

Ferrara, Orestes. *El Panamericanismo y la Opinion Europea*. Paris: Le Livre Libre, 1930.

_____. *Tentativas de Intervencion Europea en America.* Habana: Editorial Hermes, 1935.

Fitzgerald, Martin (ed.). *Sixty Milestones of Progress, 1859–1919.* Portland, Oregon: Ladd and Tilton Bank, 1919.

Ganzert, Frederic W. "The Baron Do Rio Branco, Joaquim Nabuco and the Growth of Brazilian-American Friendship, 1900–1910," *Hispanic American Historical Review,* 22 (Aug., 1942), 432–451.

Gardner, Lloyd C. "American Foreign Policy, 1900–1921: A Second Look at the Realist Critique in American Diplomacy," in *Towards A New Past: Dissenting Essays in American History,* ed. Barton J. Bernstein, New York: Pantheon, 1968.

Gil, Enrique. *Evolucion del Panamericanismo: el Credo de Wilson y el Panamericanismo.* Buenos Aires: Ed. de Jesus d Menendez, 1933.

Goldman, Eric. *Rendezvous with Destiny: A History of Modern American Reform.* New York: Knopf, 1952.

Haber, Samuel. *Efficiency and Uplift: Scientific Management in the Progressive Era, 1890–1920.* Chicago: University of Chicago Press, 1964.

Harrington, Fred Harvey. *God, Mammon and the Japanese: Dr. Horace Allen and Korean-American Relations, 1884–1905.* Madison: University of Wisconsin Press, 1944.

Hays, Samuel P. *Conservation and the Gospel of Efficiency: The Progressive Conservation Movement, 1890–1920.* Cambridge: Harvard University Press, 1959.

_____. *The Response to Industrialism, 1885–1914.* Chicago: University of Chicago Press, 1957.

Headrick, Roger L. "John Barrett: Pioneer Advocate of Practical Pan Americanism," Unpublished A. B. thesis, Williams College, 1958, filed with the John Barrett MSS, Library of Congress.

Hedges, James Blaine. *Henry Villard and the Railways of the Northwest.* New Haven: Yale University Press, 1930.

Hicks, John D. *The Populist Revolt.* Minneapolis: University of Minnesota Press, 1931.

Hill, Lawrence. *Diplomatic Relations between the United States and Brazil.* Durham: Duke University Press, 1932.

Hoffmann, Charles. "The Depression of the Nineties," *Journal of Economic History,* XVI (June, 1956), 137–164.

Hofstadter, Richard. *The Age of Reform: From Bryan to F.D.R.* New York: Knopf, 1955.

Huthmacher, J. Joseph. *Senator Robert F. Wagner and the Rise of Urban Liberalism.* New York: Atheneum, 1968.

_____. "Urban Liberalism and the Age of Reform," *Mississippi Valley Historical Review,* 49 (Sept., 1962), 231–241.

Israel, Jerry. "For God, For China and For Yale—The Open Door in Action," *American Historical Review,* LXXV (Feb., 1970), 796–807.

_____. *Progressivism and the Open Door: America and China, 1905–1921.* Pittsburgh: University of Pittsburgh Press, 1971.

Jessup, Philip C. *Elihu Root.* 2 vols. New York: Dodd, Mead & Co., 1938.

Kerr, Duncan J. *The Story of the Great Northern Railway Company and James J. Hill.* Princeton: Princeton University Press, 1939.

Kolko, Gabriel. *The Roots of American Foreign Policy.* Boston: Beacon Press, 1969.

_____. *The Triumph of Conservatism.* London: Collier-Macmillan Limited, 1963.

LaFeber, Walter. *The New Empire: An Interpretation of American Expansion, 1860–1898.* Ithaca: Cornell University Press, 1963.

Lane, George B. "The Role of John Barrett in the Development of the Pan American Union, 1907–1920," Washington, D.C.: Unpublished Ph.D. dissertation, American University, 1962.

Leopold, Richard. *Elihu Root and the Conservative Tradition.* Boston: Little, Brown & Co., 1954.

Leuchtenburg, William E. "Progressivism and Imperialism: The Progressive Movement and American Foreign Policy, 1898–1916," *Mississippi Valley Historical Review,* XXXIX (Dec., 1952), 483–504.

Levine, Daniel. *Varieties of Reform Thought.* Madison: State Historical Society of Wisconsin, 1964.

Link, Arthur S. *Woodrow Wilson and the Progressive Era, 1910–1917.* New York: Harper & Bros., 1954.

Lobo, Helio. *O Pan-Americanismo eo Brazil.* Sao Paulo: Eds. da Companhia Ed. Nacional, 1939.

Lockey, Joseph B. *Pan Americanism: Its Beginnings.* New York: Macmillan, 1920.

Luquin, Eduardo. *La Politica Internacional de la Revolucion Constitucionalists.* Mexico City: Instituo Nacional de Estudios Historicos de la Revolucion Mexicana, 1957.

McCormick, Thomas J. *China Market: America's Quest for Informal Empire, 1893–1901.* Chicago. Quadrangle, 1967.

Martin, James V. "A History of the Diplomatic Relations between Siam and the United States, 1833–1929," Medford, Mass.: Unpublished Ph.D. dissertation, Fletcher School of Law and Diplomacy, 1947.

Martin, Percy A. *Latin America and the War.* Baltimore: Johns Hopkins Press, 1925.

Maurtua, Anibal. *La Idea Pan Americana.* Lima: Imprenta La Industria, 1901.

May, Ernest R. *American Imperialism: A Speculative Essay.* New York: Atheneum, 1968.

May, Ernest R. *Imperial Democracy: The Emergence of America as a Great Power.* New York: Harcourt, Brace & World, 1961.

Mecham, J. Lloyd. *A Survey of United States-Latin American Relations.* Boston: Houghton Mifflin, 1965.

_____. *The United States and Inter-American Security, 1889–1960.* Austin: University of Texas Press, 1961.

Mowry, George. *The California Progressives.* Berkeley: University of California Press, 1951.

Munro, Dana G. "American Commercial Interests in Manchuria," *Tne Annals,* XXXIX (Jan. 1912), 154–168.

Muzzey, David Saville. *James G. Blaine: A Political Idol of Other Days*. New York: Dodd, Mead & Co., 1934.

Nabuco, Carolina. *The Life of Joaquim Nabuco*. trans. Ronald Hilton. Palo Alto: Stanford University Press, 1950.

Naudon de la Sota, Carlos. *America Impaciente*. Santiago de Chile: Ed. del Pacifico, 1963.

Nearing, Scott and Joseph Freeman. *Dollar Diplomacy: A Study of American Imperialism*. New York: Huebsch, 1925.

Nixon, Raymond B. *Henry W. Grady: Spokesman of the New South*. New York: Knopf, 1943.

Noble, David. *The Progressive Mind, 1890-1917*. Chicago: Rand McNally & Co., 1970.

Noble, David. "The Religion of Progress in America, 1890-1914," *Social Research*, 22 (Winter, 1950), 417-440.

Oliveira Lima, Manuel de. *Pan Americanismo*. Rio de Janeiro: Garnier, 1907.

Parrini Carl P. *Heir to Empire: United States Economic Diplomacy, 1916-1923*. Pittsburgh: University of Pittsburgh Press, 1969.

Pereyra, Carlos. *La Doctrina de Monroe: el Destino Manifesto y el Imperialismo*. Mejico: Ballesca, 1908.

Perkins, Dexter. *Hands Off: A History of the Monroe Doctrine*. Boston: Little, Brown & Co., 1942.

––––––. *The United States and Latin America*. Baton Rouge: Louisiana State University Press, 1961.

Peterson, Gustav H. "Latin America: Benign Neglect Is Not Enough," *Foreign Affairs*, LI (April, 1973), 598-607.

Prisco, Salvatore III. "A Vermonter in Siam: How John Barrett Began His Diplomatic Career," *Vermont History* XXXVII (Spring, 1969), 83-93.

––––––. "John Barrett and Oregon Commercial Expansion, 1889-1898," *Oregon Historical Quarterly*, LXXI (June, 1970), 141-160.

––––––. "John Barrett, Exponent of Commercial Expansion: A Study of a Progressive Era Diplomat, 1887-1920," New Brunswick, New Jersey: Unpublished Ph.D. dissertation, Rutgers University, 1969.

––––––. "John Barrett's Plan to Mediate the Mexican Revolution," *The Americas*, XXVII (April, 1971), 413-425.

Rippy, J. Fred. *The United States and Mexico*. New York: F. S. Crofts & Co., 1931.

Rivera, Alberto Arroyo. "La no Intervencion in el Derecho Internacional Americano," Mexico City: Unpublished law thesis, National University of Mexico, 1962.

Roa, Jorge. *Los Esados Unidas y Europea en Hispano America: Interpretacion Politica y Economica de la Doctrina Monroe, 1823-1933*. Habana: Carasa, 1935.

Robinson, Edgar E. and Victor West. *The Foreign Policy of Woodrow Wilson, 1913-1917*. New York: Macmillan, 1917.

Safford, Jeffrey. "The United States Merchant Marine and American Commercial Expansion, 1860-1920," New Brunswick, New Jersey: Unpublished Ph.D. dissertation, Rutgers University, 1968.

Scott, James B. *The International Conferences of American States, 1889–1928.* New York: Oxford University Press, 1931.

Shaw, Albert. *International Bearings of American Policy.* Baltimore: Johns Hopkins Press, 1943.

Sherrill, Charles H. *Modernizing the Monroe Doctrine.* Boston: Houghton Mifflin Co., 1916.

Spetter, Allan B. "Harrison and Blaine: Foreign Policy, 1889–1893," New Brunswick, New Jersey: Unpublished Ph.D. dissertation, Rutgers University, 1967.

Steigerwalt, Albert K. *The National Association of Manufacturers, 1895–1914, A Study in Business Leadership.* Grand Rapids, Michigan: Dean-Hicks, 1964.

Stuart, Graham H. *Latin, America and the United States.* New York: Appleton-Century-Crofts, 1955.

Teitelbaum, Louis M. *Woodrow Wilson and the Mexican Revolution, 1913–1916.* New York: Exposition Press, 1967.

Thomas, Ann Van Wynen and A. J. Thomas. *The Organization of American States.* Dallas: Southern Methodist University Press, 1963.

Turnbull, George. *History of Oregon Newspapers.* Portland: Binfords & Mort, 1939.

Tyler, Alice Felt. *The Foreign Policy of James G. Blaine.* Minneapolis: University of Minnesota Press, 1927.

Urien, Carlos. *El Denecho de Intervencion y la Doctrina Monroe.* Buenos Aires: Peuser, 1898.

Varg, Paul A. *The Making of a Myth: The United States and China, 1897–1922.* East Lansing, Mich.: Michigan St. University Press, 1968.

Varg, Paul A. "The Myth of the China Market, 1890–1914," *American Historical Review,* LXXIII (Feb., 1968), 742–758.

_____. *Open Door Diplomat: The Life of W. W. Rockhill.* Urbana: University of Illinois Press, 1952.

Vevier, Charles. *The United States and China, 1906–1913.* New Brunswick: Rutgers University Press, 1955.

Waller, Robert A. "John Barrett: Pan-American Promoter," *Mid-America,* LIII (July, 1971), 170–189.

Weinstein, James. *The Corporate Ideal in the Liberal State, 1900–1918.* Boston: Beacon Press, 1968.

Whitaker, Arthur P. *The Western Hemisphere Idea: Its Rise and Decline.* Ithaca: Cornell University Press, 1954.

White, Morton. *Social Thought in America: The Revolt Against Formalism.* New York: Viking Press, 1949.

Wiebe, Robert. *Businessmen and Reform: A Study of the Progressive Movement.* Cambridge: Harvard University Press, 1962.

_____. *The Search for Order, 1877–1920.* New York: Hill & Wang, 1967.

Wilgus, A. Curtis. "James G. Blaine and the Pan American Movement," *Hispanic American Historical Review,* 5 (Nov., 1922), 662–708.

Williams, Benjamin H. *American Diplomacy, Policies and Practice.* New York: McGraw-Hill, 1936.

_____. *Economic Foreign Policy of the United States.* New York: McGraw-Hill, 1929.

Williams, William Appleman. *The Roots of Modern American Empire: A Study of the Growth and Shaping of Social Consciousness in a Marketplace Society.* New York: Random House, 1969.

_____. *The Shaping of American Diplomacy.* 2 vols. Chicago: Rand McNally & Co., 1956.

_____. *The Tragedy of American Diplomacy.* Cleveland: World Publishing Co., 1959.

_____. *The Contours of American History.* Cleveland: World Publishing Co., 1961.

Yepres, Jesus M. *Philosophie du Pan Americanisme et Organization de la Paix.* Neuchatel: Eds. de la Boconniere, 1945.

Young, Marilyn Blatt. *The Rhetoric of Empire: American China Policy, 1895-1901.* Cambridge: Harvard University Press, 1968.

Zabrieskie, Edward. *American-Russian Rivalry in the Far East.* Philadelphia: University of Pennsylvania Press, 1946.

Zarate, Luis C. *La No Intervencion ante el Derecho Americano.* No imprint, 1963.

INDEX

145